Textiles
the indian story

An Activity Book on Textile Traditions

talking CUB
An imprint of Speaking Tiger Books

INTACH Indian National Trust for Art and Cultural Heritage
Heritage Education and Communication Service (HECS)

Speaking Tiger Books LLP
125A, Ground Floor, Shahpur Jat, near Asiad Village, New Delhi 110 049

Developed by
Heritage Education and Communication Service (HECS)
Indian National Trust for Art and Cultural Heritage (INTACH)
71, Lodhi Estate, New Delhi -110003
Tel: 24631818, 24637172, 24632267, 24632269; Fax: 91-11-24611290
Email: hecsintach@gmail.com, intachhecs@gmail.com
Website: www.intach.org, www.youngintach.org

This edition published by Talking Cub, an imprint of Speaking Tiger Books, in association with INTACH in paperback in 2023

ISBN: 978-93-5447-616-7
eISBN: 978-93-5447-618-1

Supported by the Government of India

Heritage Education and Communication Service (HECS) of INTACH has prepared an activity book on *Textiles – The Indian Story*. This publication focusses on textiles, their weaves, embellishments, embroideries and craftspersons, as well as their significance in Indian culture.

Concept and Text Development
Purnima Datt
Vaishnavi Singh
Nanki Kaur
Smriti Malhotra

Acknowledgments
Christina Shangne
Geetika Gunjan

Editing
Vaishnavi Singh
Nanki Kaur

Illustrations
Trikaya Soni
Geetika Gunjan
Manjishtha Pahilajani
Khushali Jain
Ira Nagar
Yatindra Kumar

Design and Layout: Arrt Creations
Printed by: Pragati Printers, New Delhi-28

FOREWORD

I commend the Heritage Education and Communication team for assembling an extensive handbook on India's diverse and rich textile heritage.

The INTACH Heritage Education and Communication Division was set up in 1998 and has completed 25 years during which period it has set up a network of around 4,000 heritage clubs, trained teachers, and held campaigns and activities with schools and colleges across the length and breadth of the country.

The division creates heritage awareness among the youth with the support of over 200 chapters of INTACH spread across the country. It produces a range of resource material and publications for schools and colleges, which are also used as training tools for teachers. Its initiative of spreading INTACH's vision is disseminated through the quarterly *Young INTACH Newsletter* created for its heritage clubs. It works towards making heritage learning interesting as well as memorable in a fun and educational way.

This publication, *Textiles – The Indian Story: An Activity Book on Textile Traditions*, explores the creation, significance, and role of textiles in Indian culture. It outlines the variety of textiles found in India, the manner in which they are made, the communities involved in their making, as well as their significance in our heritage. It has a number of activities that focus on informing students about all these aspects of textiles as well as their role in traditional attire.

I congratulate Ms Purnima Datt, Principal Director of the Heritage Education and Communication Division, and her team for carrying forward INTACH's mission of heritage awareness with much enthusiasm, dedication and commitment.

I wish them the very best in all their endeavours.

Dr. Chuden T. Misra
Member Secretary
Indian National Trust for Art and Cultural Heritage (INTACH)

August 2023

CONTENTS

Textiles
the indian story

*"The romance of Indian textiles lies in the subtlety,
the textures, the hues and the myriad variety of patterns
that can be woven by a simple pair of hands,
a concentrated and almost meditative mind,
and a creative spirit that traverses centuries."*

Jaya Jaitly, *Crafts Atlas of India*

DID YOU KNOW?

The Priest King sculpture of Mohenjo-daro has the trefoil leaf pattern on the cloth draped around one shoulder.

"In the Rig Veda and the Upanishads the universe is envisioned as a fabric woven by the gods. The cosmos, the ordered universe, is one continuous fabric with its warp and woof making a grid pattern."

Stella Kramrisch

Textiles - The Indian Story

Textiles have the oldest tale to tell, and India's textile tale consists of many diverse layers that have been impacted by historical, religious, and societal events over centuries. Indian textiles have crossed oceans and travelled all over, clothing people across the world. They have been traded amongst numerous countries, going far and wide, attaining religious and sacred notions too. Here we shall share their story...

The remnants of Indian textile traditions are found in the excavations of Harappa and Mohenjo-daro, of the Harappan Civilisation, which dates back to 5,000 years. The presence of moths that produced wild silk has been discovered, while Indian cotton threads wrapped around silver pots and dyed fabrics have been excavated in Mohenjo-daro. This reflects knowledge of weaving and great understanding of colour mixing in the artisans of that period.

During the Vedic period, textile traditions are mentioned in various Indian scriptures. The *Rigveda* has different names for male and female weavers, while the *Arthasashtra* mentions the distribution of raw material to spinners and weavers.

The *Mahabharata* mentions silk fabrics gifted to Yudhisthira which were called *Chitra Vastra*. Textiles such as linen (*khoman*), cotton (*kappasikam*), and silk (*kosseyam*) are mentioned in Buddhist literature too.

In the Gupta period, textile traditions flourished and attained great heights. Ajanta paintings showcase the glorious textiles worn by the people. The process of cotton cultivation has also been shown in one of the paintings!

Kanjivaram silks were developed under the patronage of the Pallava dynasty in South India in the 6th century.

In the 13th-14th century, merchants like Marco Polo wrote about Indian indigo found in the regions of Gujarat and the Malabar coast. He mentioned the finest cotton muslins and the delicate art of Indian embroidery.

During the Medieval period, courts patronised the craft of making beautiful textiles which led to an increase in production and global trade.

French traveller, François Bernier, who visited India during Shah Jahan and Aurangzeb's rule mentioned, in his writings, the *karkhanas* (workshops) where the artisans wove cloth. Lahore, Agra, Patna, Dacca (currently Dhaka and Ahmedabad were all important production centres for textiles. A popular item of the time was the muslin produced in Dhaka, in present-day Bangladesh.

Some of the silk fabrics produced such as *serbandy*, *kapoornoor*, *gulbadan*, *nihal*, *tafsil* and *mushru* were blended with cotton. The purest silk was used for *patola* which was made in Patan, Gujarat.

Wool was not so predominant and was mainly manufactured in Kashmir. Later production expanded, and the important production centres were Agra, Fatehpur Sikri and Alwar.

The Kashmiri shawl was important for royalty. The wool or *pashm* for shawl weaving was from the Changthangi goat of the Ladakh region. Carpet weaving was another popular textile craft which was practiced in Agra, Lahore and Mirzapur as well as in parts of Kashmir.

DID YOU KNOW?

Muslin was known as *mulmul khas* by the Mughals. It got names such as *abrawan* (running water), *baft hawa* (woven air) and *shabnam* (evening dew).

"A hundred yards of it [muslin] can pass through the eye of the needle, so fine is its texture, and yet the point of the steel needle cannot pierce through it easily."

Amir Khusrau

DID YOU KNOW?

The Silk Route was a network between Eurasia and North Africa via sea and land routes. The Silk Route resulted in the exchange of goods, cultures, philosophy, ideas and more...

Travellers also mention Masulipatnam (currently Machilipatnam) for being the most important centre for *kalamkari*-painted fabrics. The floral designs were dominant in many fabrics.

Zardozi work practised during the Mughal period made use of pure gold and silver threads to embellish the textiles.

Kashida and *chikan* (thread-work) was also prevalent during this time. It is believed that the Mughal Queen Noor Jahan was a great patron of the *chikankari* embroidery style.

The textile industry went through major transformation during the Mughal period and also established itself in the international trade market.

Portuguese, Dutch, and English traders arrived in India and became aware of the Indian textiles, and soon, fine Indian cotton gained popularity in Europe.

The large variety of Indian calico and other types of cotton with items ranging from handkerchiefs to draperies were in demand in the European markets. They were produced in Gujarat, Bengal, and along the Coromandel Coast.

With the Industrial Revolution, the steam engine and the spinning jenny were introduced in Europe and changed the textile dynamics between both the regions. European manufacturers set up mills and started producing fabrics in large quantities. Since these machines produced spun cloth, this cloth became more affordable and in demand compared to handmade textiles from India. Due to low sales, weavers had to abandon their craft and find other occupations. With the advent of the Industrial era in Britain, industrialists transformed India into an exporter of raw material, mainly cotton.

English merchants soon realised the economic value of establishing textile mills in India. Cotton mills were established first in Bengal and then in Bombay and Ahmedabad by Indian merchants. By 1900 there were more than 190 mills in India.

DID YOU KNOW?

The word '*Zardozi*' is made up of two Persian terms, '*zar*' meaning gold and '*dozi*' meaning embroidery. It reached its zenith in India in the 17th century, under the patronage of Mughal Emperor Akbar.

"The traditions of cloth manufacture within India continue to develop, and the production of handmade textiles is flourishing... India remains the most original, creative and prolific source of textile production..."

John Gillow

The production of wool and jute went through a change in the colonial period as well. India's major jute industry was set up by the English East India Company in the Bengal region, with Calcutta being the centre. Many jute products were exported to other parts of the globe. In fact, during the two World Wars, over a billion jute sandbags were exported from Bengal to the trenches.

The British extracted raw materials from India and exported cheap alternatives. This led to a major decline of the textile sector in India. However, during the freedom struggle British-made products were boycotted and Mahatma Gandhi popularised the use of home-spun cotton, khadi, as a part of the *Swadeshi* movement.

Khadi and the *charkha*, which spins the cotton, became the nationalistic symbols of the Indian freedom struggle. During this period, clothing became an important, symbolic way to build one's own identity. Women were draping sarees in regional styles, while *dhotis* and *kurtas* spun in khadi fabric were adopted by the people to show their nationalistic spirit.

Just as the raw materials and the process of spinning have undergone changes over the years, Indian textiles have also changed and become more modern with evolved aesthetics of textile traditions.

Post Independence, various government organisations were set up such as the All India Handloom Board and the All India Khadi and Village Industries to revive age-old textile traditions and promote, encourage and support Indian weavers. The government has also introduced numerous policies, programmes, and schemes through the years to enhance and support the textile industry.

The National Institute of Design and independent studios have helped modernise the textile industry while retaining traditions, all while catering to global demand. NGOs, fashion, cinema, and media have also helped promote traditional techniques and textiles.

DID YOU KNOW?

Madras Checks are pattered fabrics that were made by a weaver community in Chennai. These checks were exported to Africa where the Kalabari community calls them '*Injiri*'. They are a part of their identity and everyday life.

"If you wear khadi worth 1 rupee, 13 annas will be paid out of that to the poor people. But if you were to buy foreign cloth that money would go out of the country."

Mahatma Gandhi

Warm-Up Activity

Begin an exploratory textile journey

Educational goals:

- Awakening to an understanding of a textile tradition.
- Recognising the importance of textile as a part of personal heritage.
- Engaging with the textile and learning about it.

My Textile Story

What does a textile mean to you? Do you have an Indian textile (*saree/dhoti/veshti/mundu/pudve/turban/kurta/shawl* etc.) that has been a part of your family? Why is it special for you? Is it a family heirloom? Write a short biography of your unique family textile and draw it in the box given.

Warp and Weft
tanna banna

"As soft and fresh as blossoms,
as light as smoke and
as delicate and transparent as the vapours of milk,
are the fabrics that flow
from the looms of the Indian weaver."

The Indian Crafts Journal, Dastkari Haat Samiti

ACTIVITY 1

Textile Trysts

Engage with your own textile heritage

Educational goals:

- Exposing students to the fascinating world of textiles.
- Familiarising students with different processes of making textiles.
- Enhancing interaction with family members and understanding the role of textiles in their lives.

How to do the activity:

- Students can go through their family cupboards and find an old textile of their liking.
- They can observe the textile and fill in the activity sheet based on their findings.
- Students can click photos and also make sketches of the embroidery, weaves, and motifs.
- Once in the classroom, the students can make a presentation of their textiles, sharing their sketches and photographs.
- They can even bring the textile heirloom to class and showcase it (do treat old textiles with care as they can be fragile).

CELEBRATING TEXTILES

National Handloom Day is celebrated throughout the country on 7th August. It commemorates the *Swadeshi Andolan* which began on this day in 1905. This movement urged Indians to wear khadi and clothes made indigenously, and to denounce foreign-made apparel. Let us protect our textile heritage!

Textile Talks

Study a selected textile

Name of the textile:____________________________

Region or State it comes from:______________________

Answer the following questions on your textile.

1. What type of Indian textile is it? (Is it a *saree*, *dupatta*, *dhoti*, *mundu*, *veshti*, etc.)

2. Give a description of the textile:

   Texture ________________________

   Colour ________________________

   Weave/ Embroidery/ Embellishment ________________

   Motifs ________________________

   Any other ________________________

3. What is the length and breadth of the textile piece? Use a measuring tape to find out its dimensions.

4. How did this textile become a part of your family? Is it your family heirloom?

5. Present condition: Good ☐ Bad ☐

6. Steps you can take to look after this textile.

   a)____________________ b)____________________

7. Observe the motifs or weaves and make sketches in the space given below:

ACTIVITY 2

Fabric Friendships

Understand the diversity of textiles

Educational goals:

- Creating awareness about local textiles.
- Understanding the diversity of textiles.
- Learning to differentiate between different kinds of textiles.
- Instilling a sense of responsibility in caring for textile heritage.

How to do the activity:

- After completion of the previous activity, students should be paired.
- Each pair can then discuss their textiles and thereafter fill up the activity sheet.
- Following this each pair can share the details of their study.
- To sum it up, the teacher should do a comparative study of the textiles.

AN IKAT JOURNEY

A great legacy of friendship exists between India and Indonesia. Indian traders moved eastwards and exchanged fabrics. The Gujarati *patolas* or *ikats* were made for the Indonesian markets too. The Indonesian motifs were taken and woven in these Gujarat *ikats* and then exported to Indonesia.

Fabric Conversations

Dialogues between two fabric friends

FEATURES	MY TEXTILE	FRIEND'S TEXTILE
Photo		
Name		
How many years has it been in your family? (Is it a family heirloom or a recent purchase)		
Material (Cotton/Silk/ Linen, etc.)		
Texture (Coarse/Soft)		
Colour		
Details (Weave/Tie-Dye/Embroidery etc.)		
Motifs/Embellishments (Draw in the boxes given)		
Use of the Textile		
Points Of Differences		
Points Of Similarities		

ACTIVITY 3

Fibre Fusions

Discover the vast world of fibres

Educational goals:

- Identifying the different kinds of fibres.
- Creating an understanding of how textiles are made from fibres.
- Learning how animal and plant fibres differ.

How to do the activity:

- Encourage students to study the textiles and identify the fibres used to create them.
- They may research on the different kinds of fibres and understand their characteristics.
- Students can look for and gather samples of fibres to appreciate them further.

ORGANIC ORIGINS

Natural fibres have been used since before history was recorded, while weaving of fabrics from natural fibres has existed in India since 3500 BCE. Natural fibres are classified according to their origin – plant or animal. Plant fibres are further divided according to the parts of the plant they are derived from (stem, bark, root, leaf, flower, seeds, grass, and husk). Animal fibres are usually extracted from hair, fur and cocoons of worms.

DID YOU KNOW?

Mulmul khas is a very fine kind of muslin with a high thread count. Some other kinds are *khassa, jamdani,* and *dooria.* It is said that a 50m fabric could be squeezed into a matchbox!

Fibre Findings

Each fibre is unique

FIBRE	SOURCE	TEXTILE OR PRODUCT
SILK		
COTTON		
JUTE		
FLAX		
HEMP		
WOOL		

Fun with Fibres

Paste a sample of a plant fibre on the left and one of an animal fibre on the right, and write about some of their unique qualities.

Plant Fibre:

Animal Fibre:

Unique qualities of my selected fibres:

ACTIVITY 4

Thread - *Twist and Twirl*

Unravel the versatility of threads

Educational goals:

- Identifying the different kinds of threads used.
- Recognising the many purposes of a single thread.
- Understanding the base material for textiles - a thread.
- Learning the art of creativity with a thread.

How to do the activity:

- Students visit a local market and observe products in the market which use threads.
- Students then write down the names of the threads they see and how each of them is used.
- They can pick up samples of these products and bring them to school.
- They can make a friendship band using various kinds of threads.

SUTRA STORY

Sutras are collections of short ancient sayings, teachings or rules, written by early Hindu, Buddhist and Jain scholars. They are named after the thread which is used to bind them since the Sanskrit word for 'thread' is *sutra*, thereby proving how important the thread was in early India!

Thread Survey

Recognise the role of threads

Study the images and write down the product names and suggest the threads which could be used to make them.

Product:
Thread:

Product:
Thread:

Product:
Thread:

Product:
Thread:

Write a few lines on a story or unique fact associated with any one thread of your choice.

Fusion Band

- Make your own innovative band using threads, beads, sequins and glitter.
- Take five threads from different fibres.
- Braid or tie knots of all the threads together in an interesting design using buttons, beads, sequins, etc. Gift your handmade fusion band to your friends!

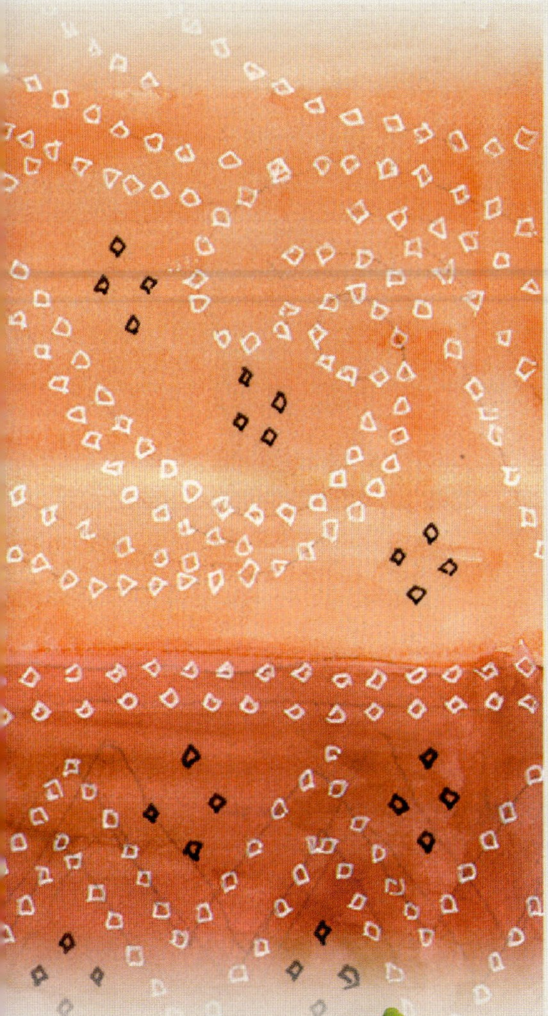

ACTIVITY 5

Dyes Naturally

Make your own colours

Educational goals:

- Exposing the students to natural colours or dyes and how they can be made at home.
- Promoting better understanding of plant-based natural extracts and their multipurpose uses.
- Learning about the making of colours and the process followed to dye a fabric.

How to do the activity:

- Students can make their own dye using natural colours.
- They can be divided into groups and asked to make dyed fabrics using our step-by-step technique.
- Students should research about the indigo plant and its role in the Indian freedom struggle.

ANCIENT COLOURS

Blue or ***neel*** of the indigo plant is the earliest known colour in the world. It was used to prepare shades of blue colour to dye fabric.

Shades of **red** and **brown** are made from the madder plant, one of the oldest dyes. Cotton textiles discovered from the Harappan Civilisation dating to around 3000 BCE are of reds, orange-red, and terracotta colours.

Yellow colour was prepared from turmeric roots and marigold flowers. To obtain darker shades, pomegranate peels and the outermost layer of onions were added to the dye.

Black colour was obtained by mixing black charcoal and iron minerals. Later, tamarind bean paste was added to the solution of rusted iron mixed with molasses to get a dark colour.

Green colour was obtained by applying tints of yellow over the base of indigo blue.

Colour the Fabric

Explore the world of natural dyes

Students can make their own natural dyes and colour their fabrics.

Follow the instructions given below to dye your fabric.

1. Place the plant material in a large stainless steel bowl and fill the bowl with twice the portion of water as the plant material. (For example: green from spinach, yellow from turmeric, brown from tea/coffee, orange from onion skins, etc)
2. Boil it until it has a dark colour then strain out the plant material before returning the liquid to the pot and placing the fabric in the pot.
3. Slow boil the fabric for an hour and then let it sit in the pot for some time or even overnight to get a darker hue of the colour.
4. Take out the fabric from the pot, wash it with cold water and dry as usual.

Experiment with varied colours

Use the following steps to make your own multi-coloured tie and dye product.

1. After making the colours using the above mentioned method try and use two or three different dyes on your fabric.
2. Take a white cotton shirt and using rubber bands, tie and twirl to create designs.
3. Fill the colours in different tube bottles and colour the sections of tied shirt in any way you want.
4. Let it dry naturally overnight and wash it in cold water. Paste a cut-out of your product in the given space.

DID YOU KNOW?

The Champaran Satyagraha was a major event in the Indian freedom movement where farmers were protesting against the forced cultivation of indigo.

ACTIVITY 6

Weaving Wisdom

Understand how fabric is woven

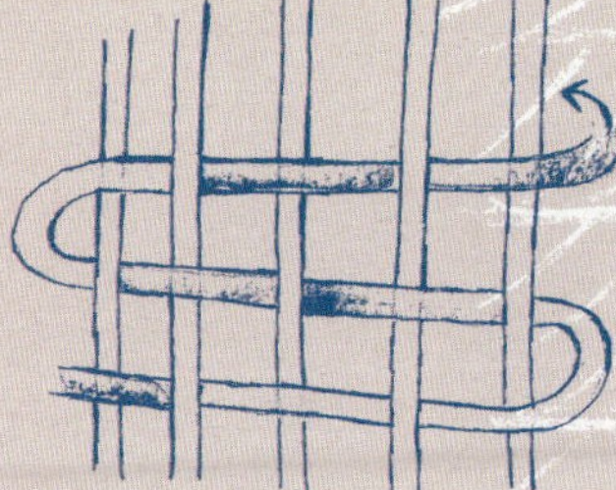

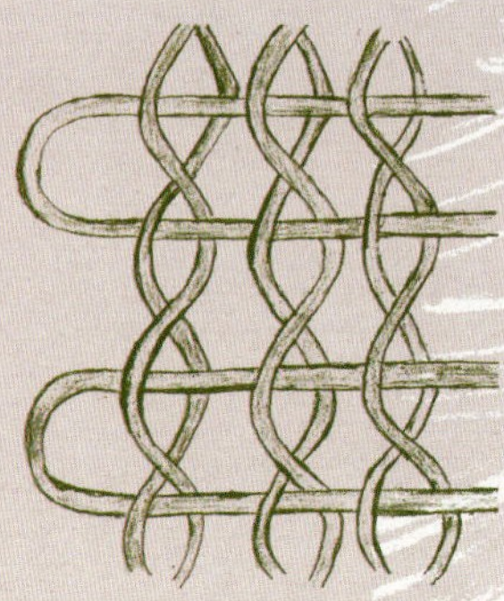

Educational goals:

- Learning what a weave is.
- Identifying the kinds of weaving techniques.
- Recognising the differences in weaves.
- Understanding the method of making a woven pattern.

How to do the activity:

- Students can select textiles or fabrics from their wardrobe or pick up samples from the local market.
- They must find out the weaving styles of the selected pieces and research on the weaving process.
- They should attempt to create their own products using these methods.
- They can visit a local artisan and observe the way in which textiles are woven. After their visit they can have a discussion about their experience and learning in the classroom.

KINDS OF WEAVES

Plain Weave
Single weft yarns go alternatively under and over each warp yarn.

Satin Weave
Four or more weft yarns go over one warp yarn and vice versa.

Basket Weave
Two or more yarns are used at a time to create the same plain weave.

Twill Weave
The weft is passed over and under two or more warp yarns, shifting it by one on each row.

Warp and Weft

Create your own weave

Step 1: Take 2 pages of paper and paint them in two different colours, or take coloured paper. Choose one as your weft (vertical) and one as your warp (horizontal).

Step 2: Take the page chosen as the weft and fold it in half. Draw a single one-inch wide line horizontally at the top. Draw 8 equal vertical lines on it, and cut along these lines until you reach the horizontal line and stop.

Step 3: Take your warp page and fold it in half. Draw 8 equal vertical lines and cut along these lines. You should cut all the way in this one to make long strips of paper.

Step 4: Unfold both the pages of the paper and start weaving. Starting at the bottom, weave a paper strip (warp) over and then under, through the weft paper.

Step 5: For the next paper strip, start weaving in the opposite way (first under and then over). Repeat Step 4 and 5 alternately to make sure a weave is created.

Step 6: Once you have your weaving complete, you can either cut off the ends of the weave or fold them over and tape them down.

Woven Words

Sufi poet Kabir wrote these beautiful lines as a metaphor, equating life with weaving –

"I have run mere cotton threads for the warp and weft.
But how did God, the Master Weaver, make this finely woven fabric we call skin that we wear all our lives?"

Explain these lines, highlighting the metaphor.

DID YOU KNOW?

Drawing Parallels

"The loom is the weaver's instrument and...when the weaver fills his bani or weft and throws his shuttle, it is as if the musician started the alap. And like a raga, weaving has a certain laya or rhythm."

Harsha V Dehejia

ACTIVITY 7

Myriad Looms

Explore looms and their working

Educational goals:

- Becoming aware of different types of looms.
- Understanding the working of various kinds of looms.
- Creating awareness about endangered hand-woven fabrics.

How to do the activity:

- Students visit a weaving cluster or village.
- They can interact and interview craftspersons and note their observations.
- Students can then discuss their learnings from the loom survey with their peers in the classroom.

Tree loom

Loin loom

Pit loom

Ground loom

TYPES OF LOOMS

Tree loom: In this loom, one end of the loom is tied to a tree as support to keep the warp tight.

Loin loom: In this, one end of the loom has a band which is fixed around the weaver's torso to make the yarn taut.

Draw loom: This has two sets of shafts or harnesses which make it possible to create intricate patterns in weaves easily.

Pit loom: Four posts are sunk into the ground, over a pit. The warp is operated with a paddle in the pit.

Warp-weighted loom: This rectangular loom has warp yarns running vertically. The weaver stands in front of the loom to insert the weft.

Ground loom: The poles of the loom are put into the ground at a distance equal to the required width of the fabric being made.

Loom Logic

Try and make a simple loom of your own

- Take a cardboard piece of any size
- Leave 1 inch from the sides and mark every ¼ inch section on both the top and the bottom of the piece horizontally and vertically
- Cut at the markings
- Insert a warp thread/ribbon
- Start weaving!

Loom Survey

Observe and answer

Visit a handloom textile centre/workshop/*haat*/fair in your city, region, or state. In particular, let us study the use of hand or semi-mechanised looms, and understand the process. Answer the questions below after you return from your visit.

1. Which textiles are made at the site you visited?

____

2. What kind of loom/s are used to make these textiles?

____

3. How many people work on the looms, and for how long have they been working there?

____

4. Is this work hereditary and if so from when has his/her family been working on this craft?

____

5. How long does it take to weave one saree or a piece of textile?

____

6. Describe and sketch the loom you saw at the site.

____

____

____

____

____

ACTIVITY 8

Fabric Creations

Learn about the steps in the making of textiles

Educational goals

- Understanding the cycles of production for cotton and silk fabrics.
- Appreciating the work by craftspersons.
- Learning about the stages in the making of textiles from various kinds of fibres.

How to do the activity:

- Students must watch videos of how cotton/silk is made and note down their observations.
- Students should learn and share the production cycle of other natural fibres like jute, flax etc.

AHIMSA SILK

Ahimsa or non-violent silk was created to not harm or kill the silkworms in the process of extracting silk. The cocoon is left alone for 7-10 days and once the worms grow inside the cocoon, they pierce the cocoon and fly away as moths. It is often referred to as peace silk as it is processed without the killing of silkworms.

DID YOU KNOW?

India's major jute industry was set up by the British East India Company in the Bengal region, with Calcutta being the centre. After the Partition of 1947, most of the jute-producing land went to East Pakistan (now Bangladesh), while the mills were in India. Jute then started being produced in West Bengal and other parts of eastern India.

Magical Movements

Let's learn the process

COTTON

COTTON PICKING
Cotton seeds with fibres are picked from the pod manually. Along with that, a lot of organic matter like dried leaves, hay etc. gets collected.

GINNING & COMBING
Through cleaning and drying, the impurities are removed either manually or using devices, and the cotton fibre is combed and straightened.

SPINNING
Spinning is the process of turning fibres into yarns. Cotton fibres with their natural twist can be spun with hands or using spindles and spinning wheels.

DYEING
The yarn is coloured using dyes or pigments to obtain the desired colour in the fabric.

WEAVING

Weaving in India is majorly done on looms, which are frames that hold the warp threads tightly for the length of the intended fabric. The warp threads are then crossed with weft threads at a right angle, thus forming a weave.

SILK

REARING SILKWORMS
Silk is procured from the cocoons of silkworms. The first step involves keeping the silkworm eggs at 65ºF and gradually increasing the temperature to 77ºF.

HATCHING OF SILKWORMS

The baby worms are then fed mulberry leaves every half an hour. Within one month the worms increase 10,000 times their size.

COCOON STAGE

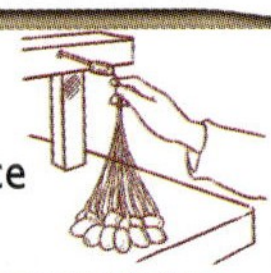

It takes the worms 3-4 days to build the cocoons by producing a jelly-like substance which hardens on contact with air.

BOILING COCOONS
The worms are separated from the cocoons which are then dried for 8-9 days. The cocoons are then dipped in hot water to loosen the filament.

REELING, SPOOLING AND WEAVING
Each cocoon filament is 600-900 metres long. Five to eight of these make a strong thread. They are put together on a spooling frame to make them stronger. These are finally woven.

Flax Findings

It is believed that flax, the fibre used to make linen, was cultivated in India over 5,000 years ago. It is the earliest known vegetable fibre to be woven and worn. Linen and flax have been mentioned in ancient Hindu scriptures and Jain texts.

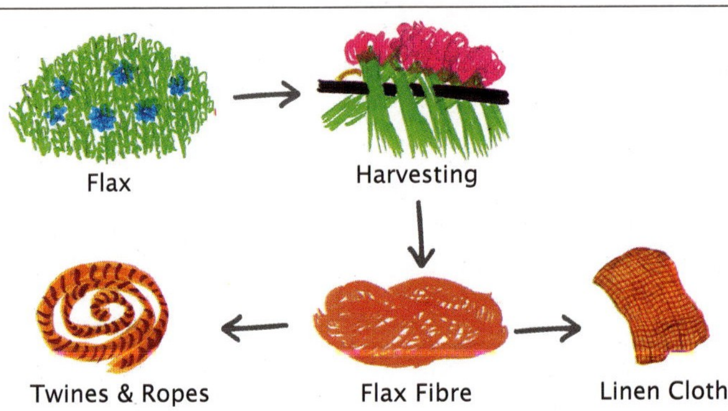

Show us in the space below the cycle of jute/ wool/ any other natural fibre from the source to the weave.

ACTIVITY 9

Khadi: Fabric of Freedom

Dwell into the world of khadi

Educational goals:

- Making students aware of the significance of khadi.
- Understanding the role of khadi in our history and society.
- Enlightening students about the benefits of sustainable products.

How to do the activity:

- Make the students learn the art of spinning by making their own thread on the *charkha*.
- Learn about the use of khadi by Gandhiji in India's freedom struggle.
- Make your own personal diary on khadi.
- List down important qualities of khadi, bringing out its sustainable features.
- Debate on the topic: 'Khadi: An Eco-Friendly Fabric and its Health Benefits.'

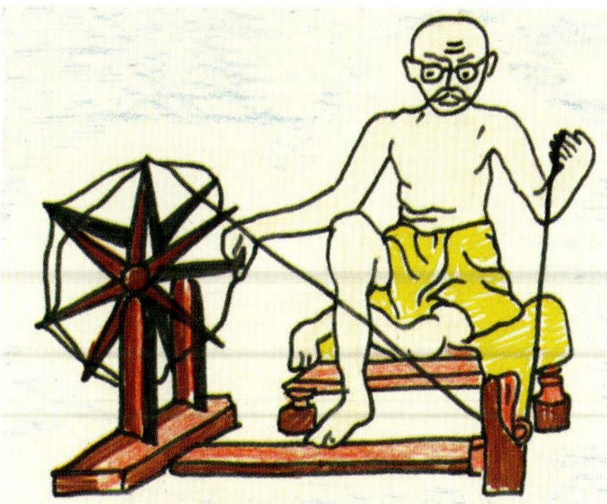

GANDHI AND THE ROLE OF KHADI

Khadi was a part of a whole movement started by Mohandas Karamchand Gandhi. This was called the Swadeshi movement, which aimed at boycotting foreign goods. Gandhiji promoted khadi for rural self-employment and self-reliance. No wonder Gandhiji concluded that "for every minute I spin a thread, is in me the consciousness that I am adding to the nation's wealth."

DID YOU KNOW?

The *Charkha* was chosen as the symbol of Swaraj by Mahatma Gandhi. It was also one of the early symbols that featured on the national flag.

Khadi: The Unique Fabric

Charkha Time!

Try your hand at spinning the *charkha* and produce your own thread. Visit a Gandhi Museum/Ashram or a khadi village nearby and experience the *charkha*.

Khadi spinning at INTACH Headquarters

Khadi's Personal Diary

Khadi writes about her experience with Gandhiji in her diary. She shares her importance in India's freedom struggle. Continue this letter describing khadi's journey in India.

Dear Diary,
Tears of joy roll down when I remember those days which I spent with Bapu. I am a hand-spun and hand-woven cloth made out of cotton. But in India I am not just a cloth. I was started as a movement. Bapuji promoted an ideology that Indians can be self-reliant on cotton...

Jai Hind,
Khadi

Khadi: A Sustainable Fabric

Khadi is eco-friendly because it decomposes in the earth within six months.
It is also comfortable to wear and does not irritate the skin like synthetic clothes.
Mention other sustainable qualities of khadi.

ACTIVITY 10

Masterful Motifs

Understand the motifs of textiles

Educational goals:

- Looking at motifs and unique patterns.
- Learning about the meaning of various motifs.
- Understanding the diversity of designs.
- Appreciating the beauty of Indian motifs and designs.

How to do the activity:

- Students are requested to bring a piece of textile from their home to school.
- They can study the different motifs on the textile and describe the details.
- They must examine the motifs and designs and see if there is a story that is being expressed by the weaver in the textile.
- They then learn about the motifs and their significance and can have a discussion about it in class.

MOTIF MEANINGS

Ambi:
Paisley or the *ambi* motif is one of the most popular motifs in India which signifies fertility and life.

Peacock:
This motif is common in many Indian textiles. It represents immortality, courtship and fertility.

Tree of Life:
The Banyan and Peepal trees are popularly depicted in Indian textiles. Their roots are the base or foundation of life.

Lotus:
This is an important motif and one of the oldest sacred symbols found in Indian textiles. The lotus symbolises cosmic balance.

Make a Motif

Design your own textile motifs

In the graphs below make two designs, one with a single motif and one with a repetitive motif.

Unique Motifs

Write down the significance of the following motifs in a line or two and mention the textiles they are found on:

1. Tree of Life

2. Elephant

3. Palanquin

4. Temple gopura

Make some unique motifs by seeking inspiration from our traditional motifs.

Traditional Motifs	My Motifs

ACTIVITY 11

Incredible Ikats

Unravel the world of Ikats

Educational goals:

- Understanding the process and design patterns of an *ikat* textile.
- Learning about the different kinds of *ikat* textiles.
- Becoming aware of the community associated with *ikat* making.
- Tracing the history and travels of this textile across the globe.

How to do the activity:

- Students can collect different kinds of *ikats*.
- They can then find out the significance of the motifs made in *ikats* such as in Sambalpuri *ikats*, *patola*, etc.
- Students may speak to an *ikat* weaver and have a dialogue regarding the making of this textile.
- Find out the cultural significance of *ikats* in different countries.

INDIA'S IKATS

Pochampally Ikat: These come from a region of the same name in Telangana. The beginnings of this *ikat* style can be traced to the weaving of the *telia rumal*. Traditional motifs and geometric patterns are woven within the textile, in both cotton and silk.

Patola: These double *ikat* silk textiles come exclusively from Patan, Gujarat. They have been exported to Indonesia where they were ceremonially used. Traditional *patola* designs are elephants, tigers, parrots, etc.

Sambalpuri Ikat: These cotton and silk *ikats* are different from the Gujarati version. This textile tradition has weaving centres in Nuapatna, Sambalpur and Sonepur in Odisha. The motifs represented on them are generally fish, animals, or florals designs.

DID YOU KNOW?

Telia Rumal is a double *ikat* fabric from Chirala, Andhra Pradesh. '*Telia*' means 'oil' and '*Rumal*' means 'handkerchief'. It was worn by fisherman as the oil in the fabric did not let the salt water seep through.

Ikat Impressions

Try your hand at making an Ikat woven textile

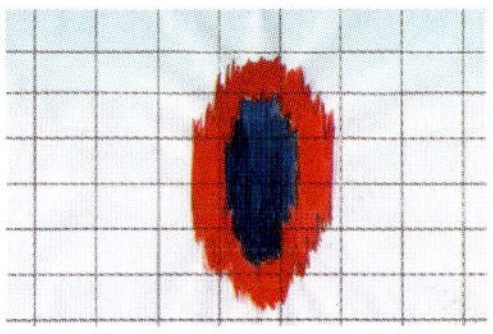

Ikat design

Make your own ikat impression

- While professionals can easily weave beautiful *ikat* designs, you can try your hand at it too.
- Look at some *ikat* sarees to understand the design. Take a sheet and draw a grid on it.
- Create a design in a similar style, using the grid for assistance.
- To give it a blurry look, like in the weave, make sure that you make up and down lines instead of straight ones. (Irregular alignment of dyed yarns causes a slight mismatch of threads which results in the blurry effect of the *ikat* design).

See the pictures below to understand the process of weaving!

Step 1 Dyeing

Step 2 Drying

Step 3 Spinning

Step 4 Putting Yarn on the Loom

Step 5 Weaving

Ikat Journeys

Patan Patola Heritage Museum houses 200-year-old heirlooms and samples of *ikat* textiles from countries like Thailand, Uzbekistan, Philippines and Indonesia. Started by the Salvi family, they are carrying forward the legacy of making this textile since the 11th century.

On the world map, highlight countries other than India where different varieties of *ikat* are found.

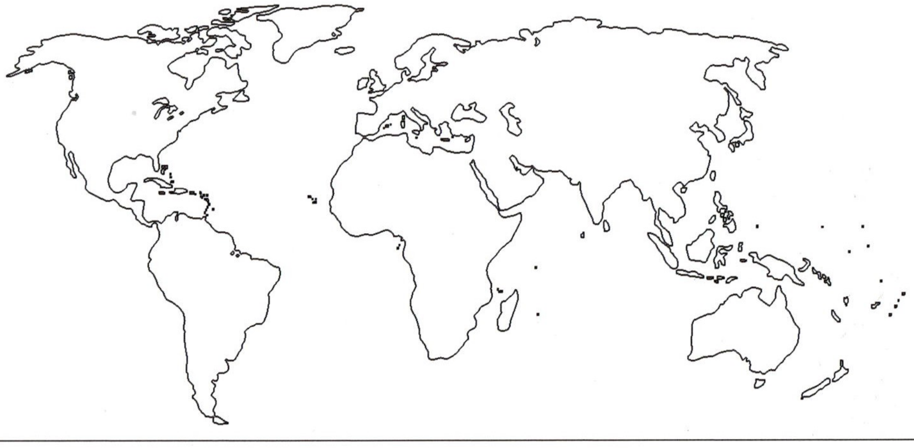

ACTIVITY 12

Captivating Kanjivaram

Study the intricate pattern of Kanjivaram silks

Educational goals:

- Learning about different *Kanjivaram* weaves.
- Exploring the range of traditional weaving practices.
- To be able to distinguish between different *Kanjivaram* saree weaves.
- Understanding the motifs and patterns used on the sarees.

How to do the activity:

- Students can learn about the history of *Kanjivaram* saree and draw any temple design of their choice.
- They can understand the steps involved in the making of the saree and paste it in their notebooks.
- They may understand the nature of the weaving process and what the design patterns indicate.

KNOW THE KANJIVARAM

Based on the yarn, weaves, and border style, *Kanjivaram* sarees are of four types. These sarees have mainly originated in Kanchipuram.

Plain Weave
Plain saree with gold borders

Traditional Weave
Heavy saree with motifs of coin, *chakra* and checks

Temple Weave
Zigzag and temple designs or *gopurams* at the border

Floral Weave
Intricate floral design with plain gold borders

Temple Template

Draw a temple design

DID YOU KNOW?

Kanjivaram weavers are believed to be the descendants of Sage Markanda, who was the master weaver for the Gods.

Kanjivaram Katha

Steps of making a *Kanjivaram* saree are given below. Cut and paste each step in your note-book and paste pictures of any 3 steps as well.

Thread Extraction
Raw silk from mulberry and silkworms is needed for weaving. The extracted yarns are then dipped in rice water and dried in sunlight to make it thick and stiff.

Twisting
The raw silk is twisted to produce warp and weft threads. This saree is thick so it requires more warp threads in comparison to other silk sarees.

Dyeing
The warp and weft threads are then dyed with required colours and the process of dyeing is done by hand.

Degumming
The threads are thoroughly washed and soaked in boiling water to remove the gum or starch from the threads.

Designing
The next stage is that of selecting the design. The colours and motifs are decided too.

Warping and *zari* work
In warping, each warp thread is placed in the loom. The *zari* borders are also woven in the loom with silver and gold thread.

Weaving
The warp and weft threads are placed in a shuttle to produce the weave. The *Kanjivaram* saree has three parts - body, border and *pallu* and the saree is joined by the interlocking process. Finally emerges a beautiful *Kanjivaram* saree!

ACTIVITY 13

Brilliant Banarasi

Discover the beauty of Banarasi brocades

Educational goals:

- Identifying the material heritage of silk brocades.
- Recognising the rich and varied motifs of the Banarasi brocade weave.
- Understanding the designs for brocade textiles.
- Discovering the role of the government in the development of these textiles.

How to do the activity:

- Students should find a Banarasi brocade fabric or saree at home, grandparents' home or a local market.
- They can observe its silk threads, *zari* work, and motifs carefully.
- Students then write down the names of the motifs seen.
- They may research on the GI tags associated with some textiles.

BANARASI BROCADES

Banarasi brocades are intricate fabrics woven out of silk and threads of gold and silver known as *zari*. The *naqsha* (plan/map/pattern) and *naqshabandi* (designer) are two extremely vital parts of a brocade fabric. *Kinkhab*, a heavy fabric, is the most famous brocade textile of Banaras.

OTHER BROCADES

India is a land of brocades, with each region having its own variations. One of the earliest recorded examples of brocade weaving comes from Ahmedabad, Gujarat. Other iconic variations of brocades include *Paithani* (Maharashtra), *Chanderi* (Madhya Pradesh), and *Baluchari* (West Bengal).

DID YOU KNOW?

The Hajong people, an ethnic tribe in North-east India, wear a brocaded shawl called Argon in winters and on special occasions. The shawl consists of symmetrical geometric designs.

Beautiful Brocade

Draw the brocade design

Study the common Banarasi brocade motifs given below such as *buti*, *buta*, *jaal*, *jangla*, and *bel* and draw a design using any two motifs!

Bel - Floral repetitive pattern

Jaal - A net-like pattern

Buti - A single motif

Buta - A larger buti

Jangla - Floral and paisley designs

GI Tag - Global Recognition

In 2009, a Geographical Indication (GI) tag was granted to the weavers of Uttar Pradesh for Banarasi sarees and brocade. Research on the geographical indications (GI) tags granted to textiles across India and fill in the table below!

TEXTILE	STATE	CHARACTERISTICS
Pashmina		
Wangkhei Phee		
Phulkari		
Chanderi		
Kanjivaram		
Kotpad		
Hmaram		
Baluchari		

ACTIVITY 14

Colourful North-East

Learn about the various weaves of the North-East

Educational goals:

- Creating awareness of regional variation in textiles of the North-east.
- Discovering the design patterns and their significance.
- Understanding the reasons for the diversity of North-eastern textiles.

How to do the activity:

- Students can be divided into pairs to do various activities related to North-eastern textiles.
- They can learn about the cultural significance of each textile and its motif and sketch the same.
- They can study how the textiles are made and do a creative activity to better understand the processes.

Lepcha

Apatani

Muga

MANIFOLD WEAVES

Lepcha, Sikkim

The *Lepcha* textile was traditionally woven with nettle yarn but is now spun from cotton and wool too. The cotton is used as a base to weave the wool in different geometric motifs.

Apatani, Arunachal Pradesh

The *Apatani* weave is characterised by a cotton weave with geometric designs. The fabric is used to weave shawls known as *jig-jiro* and *jjilan* or jackets called *supuntarii*.

Puan, Mizoram

This cotton textile is worn like a skirt by women. The body is usually white with red, green and black patterns. Different motifs like stars and flowers are woven on the *Puan*.

Muga, Assam

This is a rare yellowish-golden silk, made from the natural fibre of the semi-cultivated silkworm named *Antheraea assamensis*. The uniqueness is that its golden lustre increases with age.

Woven Wonders

Dive into the world of wonderful weaves

In North-east India, motifs on textiles have a unique significance. The Naga Warrior shawls are painted/ embroidered with figures. Complete the central band of this shawl.

Traditional Assamese, Naga and Manipuri motifs are used on various textiles. Research and discover the meaning of these motifs.

Naga weave

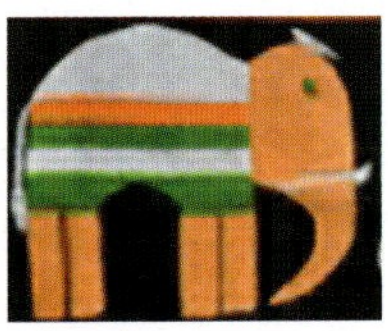

Akoybi weave

Assamese weave

Glorious Gamocha

Another glorious textile tradition that hails from Assam is the *gamocha*. Find out and write about it below.

Baluchari

Tangail

Jamdani

ACTIVITY 15

Wondrous Weaves

Engage with Bengali weaves

Educational goals:

- Studying the different variations of Bengali weaves made across the region.
- Learning the method of weaving, motif meanings and more about the woven fabric.
- Understanding age-old and traditional methods of recycling clothing items.

How to do the activity:

- Students can see samples of a variety of woven textiles from this region.
- They can have a discussion about the characteristic features of these fabrics, especially muslin.
- Students then research and find out how the Partition of India affected the textile industry in Bengal.
- They can explore the role of creative recycling in Bengal's textile.

DID YOU KNOW?

Garad silk saree is characterised by its white colour with red borders. These sarees have sacred value. They are largely made using silk which is not dyed.

POETRY OF THE LOOM

Baluchari - *Baluchari* silk sarees were originally produced in Murshidabad district and are known for the mythological depictions on the *pallu* of the saree.

Tangail - *Tangail* cotton and silk sarees are known for their highly decorative and colourful borders. These sarees are woven with extremely fine yarns which make them soft and delicate.

Jamdani - Originating in Dhaka, Bangladesh these sarees are made with muslin yarn and decorated with floral motifs.

Dhaniakhali - *Dhaniakhali* sarees are woven with threads of cotton and are characterised by contrasting-coloured borders.

Begumpuri - These are loosely woven, light-weight, translucent cotton sarees and are of deep and bright colours.

Magical Muslin

Write about the Bengali muslin using the following keywords –

DHAKA SAREE RING

MATCHBOX MUGHAL PRINCESS

LIGHT MEGHNA RIVER ARTHASHASTRA

DID YOU KNOW?

In ancient times, the upper jaw bones of a catfish were used to comb the raw yarn.

Meaningful Motifs

Here are three motifs found in the weaves of West Bengal. Taking inspiration from them, draw your own motifs in the boxes given.

Creative Recycling

Khesh weaving is done using recycled cotton sarees in Birbhum district, West Bengal. The warp is done with new yarn and the weft with recycled cloth made into yarns. The practice began in Shilpa Sadan, a vocational training centre in Santiniketan in the 1920s.

Try weaving a coaster using recycled cloth and paste its photograph here.

ACTIVITY 16

Symphony of Weaves

Discover the colourful variety of weaves

Educational goals:

- Understanding the weave variations in our country.
- Identifying local weaves and their uniqueness.
- Discovering the significance of each weave.

How to do the activity:

- Students should research on the origins of each local textile.
- They can read and share the story of each weave style.
- Students should visit a local cloth market, go through family cupboards or search online for the different kind of weaves.

INTACH AND TEXTILES

INTACH's Architectural Heritage Division, together with the Heritage Craft and Community Division, has been working towards the conservation of vernacular architecture in traditional weaving clusters and documenting weaving traditions. The Material Heritage Division restores textiles - from votive textiles, sarees, dupattas, to even flags!

INDIAN WEAVERS BY SAROJINI NAIDU

"Weavers, weaving at break of day,
why do you weave a garment so gay? ...
Blue as the wing of a halcyon wild,
we weave the robes of a new-born child."

People adorn various clothes during different phases of life. Read the poem and write about the different kinds of clothes that people wear through their life. Write a four-line poem on any one kind of clothing worn in our lifetime.

Varied Weaves

Share these woven wonders

Research on the weaves mentioned below, learn about them, and paste a photograph of each weave in the space given.

Name	State	Description	Photograph
Chanderi	Madhya Pradesh	This weave is used to mainly make sarees out of silk and cotton.	
Maheshwari	Madhya Pradesh	Colourful silk sarees that are woven in the town of Maheshwar.	
Paithani	Maharashtra	A woven silk saree characterised by a *zari* border and iconic motifs like parrots and flowers.	
Bhagalpuri	Bihar	Practiced mainly in the district of Bhagalpur, this silk weave produces fine and soft cloth.	
Bomkai	Odisha	A low-count cotton weave used to make sarees with tribal motifs.	
Mashru	Gujarat	A woven cloth made of silk and cotton. This has been described in depth in the *Ain-i-Akbari*.	
Ilkal	Karnataka	An ancient weave that is used to make silk and cotton sarees since the 8th century.	
Venkatagiri	Andhra Pradesh	A fine weave used to make cotton sarees. This has got a Geographical Indication or GI Tag.	
Kasavu	Kerala	These are white and gold woven cotton and silk sarees. They are a symbol of wealth and prosperity.	

India's Weave Spread

Find out about popular weaves of each state and cut and paste their pictures in the specific state in the map of India as shown. (Example, Madhya Pradesh - Chanderi and Maheshwari)

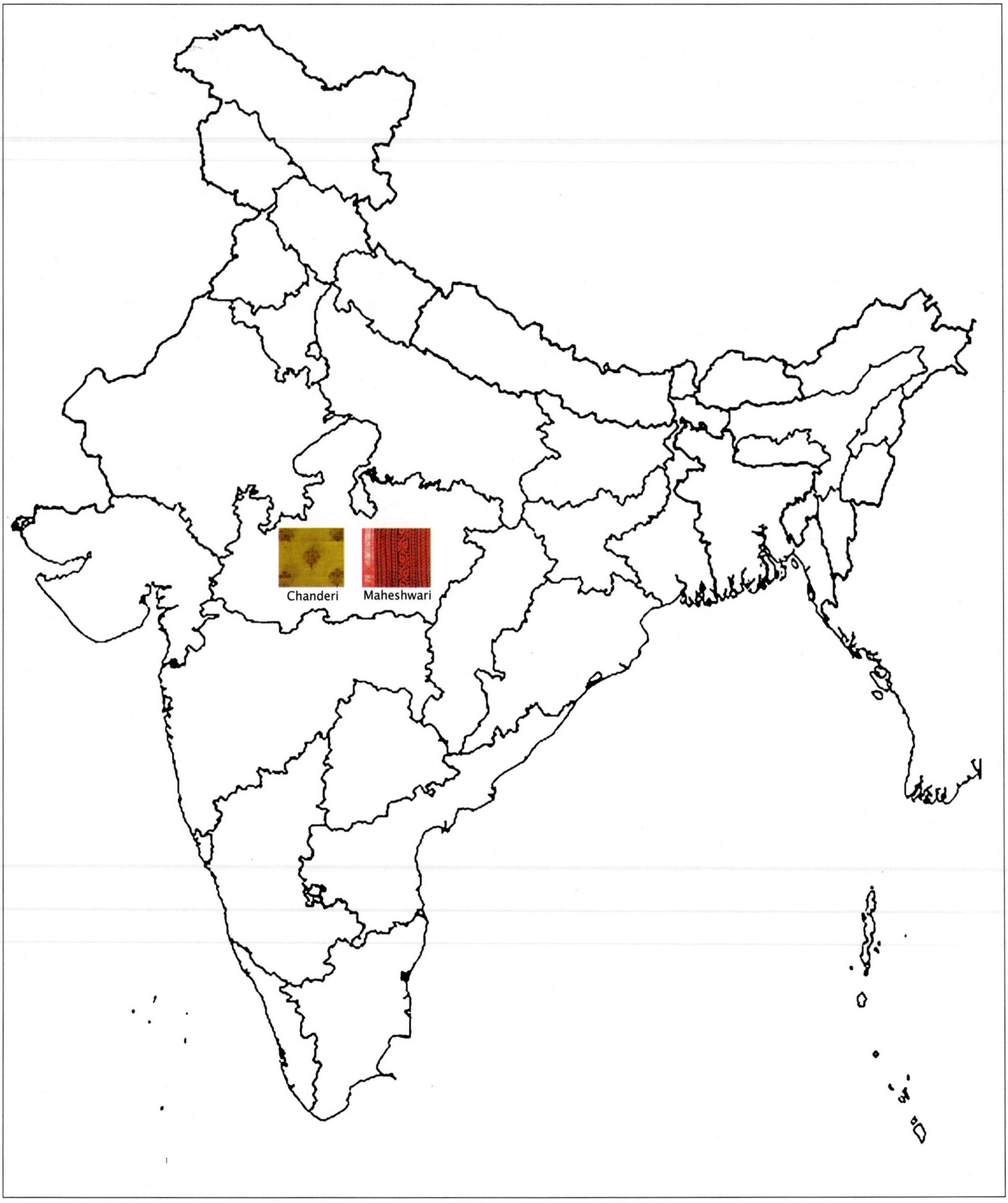

Print to Stitch
kalam kashida

"...the needle of the embroiderer,
the mould of the textile block printer,
the brush of the kalamkari maker,
the chisel of the sculptor, the kalam of the calligrapher,
the spindle of the weaver...
these are the basic tools of akritis and
are a testament to human creativity."

Harsha V Dehejia, *Akriti to Sanskriti: The Journey of Indian Forms*

ACTIVITY 1

Textile Tools

Study the tools used for textile decoration

Educational goals:

- Creating awareness of the tools used to adorn Indian fabrics.
- Identifying similarities of the tools used.
- Understanding the differences between the tools.

How to do the activity:

- Students can select any five pieces of embellished textiles from home and get them to school.
- They should then research and list down the tools used to decorate the textiles and to make the embellishments.
- They can do a creative activity using some tools.

INGENIOUS INSTRUMENTS

Block

Block is used to print on textiles, and is traditionally hand carved on wood, generally good quality *saagwan* (teak).

Kalam

Kalam (pen) is made out of pointed pieces of bamboo and is used to paint on textiles such as in *kalamkari*.

Needle

A needle is a long, thin, and pointed metal tool that is used to stitch textiles and embellish them.

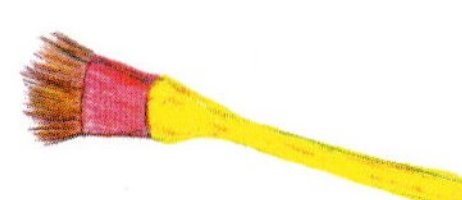

Brush

A brush can be of various sizes and materials and is used to paint designs and borders on many traditional textiles.

DID YOU KNOW?

Jara and *jhina* are specialised brushes used to paint *pichwais*. The *jara* is a broad brush made with goat hair while the *jhina* is a much thinner brush made of squirrel hair.

Tools Talk

A comparative study of some textile tools

Questions	Block	Kalam	Needle	Brush
What am I made of?				
What am I used for?				
Do I have a look-alike?				
When was I first made?				
Paste my photograph!				

Prized Pen

Make your own kalam!

Step 1: Take a small bamboo stick and sharpen one of its ends. (Please take help from an adult to do this step.)

Step 2: Roll a piece of pure cotton cloth or a lump of cotton and tie it tightly above the sharpened tip. You should tie it with a cotton thread in a criss-cross fashion to ensure it stays on properly.

Step 3: Decorate the body of the *kalam* by painting it, gluing sequins, or pasting other embellishments on it.

Step 4: Dip the cotton tip into ready-made or homemade dye and start creating your *kalamkari*.

DID YOU KNOW?

Artists use 'tamarind twigs' as pens, besides bamboo brushes to sketch the motifs on the fabric.

Paint a Tapestry

Make your own wall hanging

With the *kalam* made from the above activity, paint a cloth wall hanging.

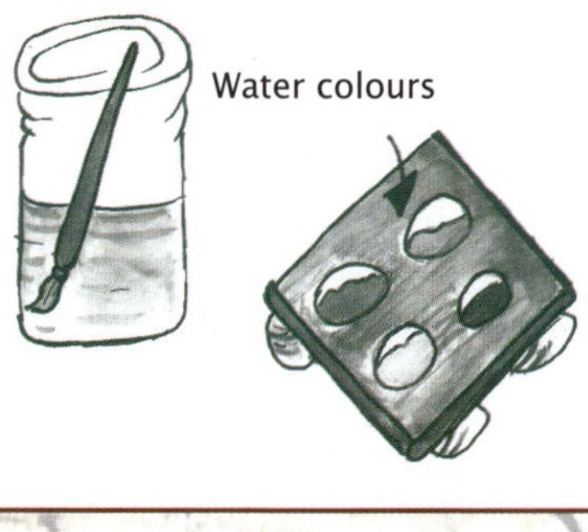

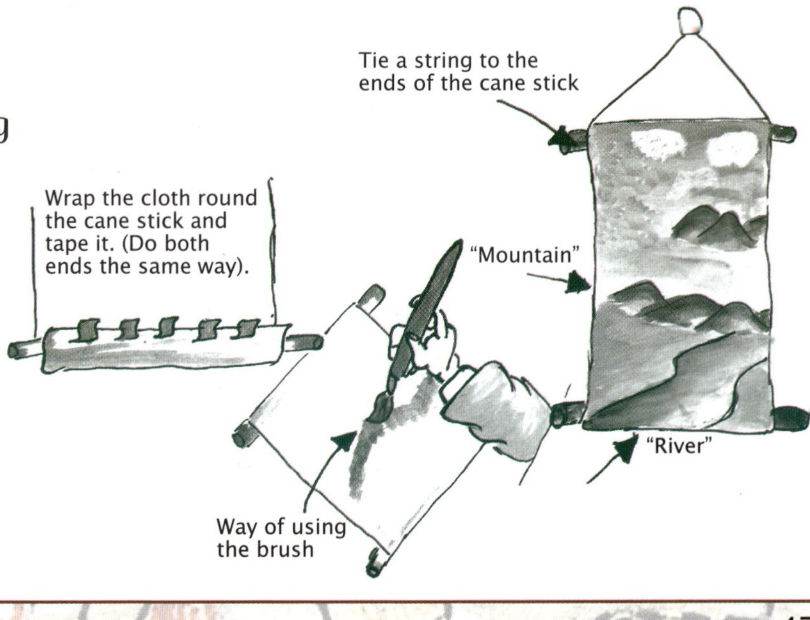

ACTIVITY 2

Precious Prints

Discover the world of block prints

Educational goals:

- Understanding and creating block designs.
- Learning how meticulously the blocks are carved and chiselled.
- Appreciating the beautiful designs that are made using these simple wooden blocks on fabric.

How to do the activity:

- Students can observe the process of block printing.
- They can also study block printed fabrics.
- Students can experiment and learn how each block and colour is used to create a design.
- Students can then bring a plain old t-shirt or *dupatta* to school to do some fun block printing.

BEAUTIFUL BLOCKS

Block printing is a traditional art of printing by pressing and stamping fabric with carved wooden blocks. The blocks are made by etching out the design on a teak or sheesham wood block. The states of Gujarat and Rajasthan are known for block prints.

MUGHAL METAPHORS

DID YOU KNOW?

The carved blocks absorb moisture during the printing process, and to prevent warping, the blocks are soaked in mustard oil for 10-15 days.

Many block printing patterns are a product of the Mughal period. These floral patterns are used as metaphors for paradise.

"Every time a wooden block touches the textile, the fabric vibrates with life. The beautiful prints on the cloth express tradition, craftsmanship and a way of life."

Anonymous

From Block to Print

Delve into the printing process

Carving & Drying →	Preparation of Colours →	Printing →	Washing
Master block carvers chisel the designs traced onto the wooden block.	The colours are prepared and kept on a tray containing glue and pigment binder to ensure a soft base for the colour, and to allow it to easily spread on the block. Natural colours were generally used earlier.	Before printing, the fabrics are washed and dried in the sun. They are then printed with blocks. After printing, the fabrics are left to dry in the sun.	Once completely dried, the fabrics are steamed and washed in water, dried in the sun again and lastly ironed.

Experimenting with Blocks

For this you will require:

- A block (you can get it in any market or use a vegetable in an innovative manner)
- The fabric to be printed (a handkerchief or a table mat, preferably white colour)
- Fabric paint/ Acrylic fabric paint
- Working table
- Pins
- Paint tray
- Newspaper

Step 1

Lay the papers on the table to avoid dirtying the table while printing.

Step 2

Place the fabric to be printed on top of the newspaper and pin it on all sides to avoid the shifting of fabric when printing is taking place.

Step3

Pour the desired paint onto the tray evenly.

Step 4

Dab the paint evenly onto the block and stamp the block on the fabric with the force of your hand. Carefully lift the block to avoid any smudging or staining of fabric.

Step 5

Continue stamping on the fabric with equal amount of pressure, keeping the designs in alignment and following the same alignment throughout for a clean artistic look.

Step 6

Once the first colour printing is finished, use the second colour filling in the blocks and subsequently all colours are printed.

Step 7

Dry the finished textile. Your very own block print textile is now ready!

ACTIVITY 3

Exquisite Embroideries

Delve into the world of embroideries

Educational goals:

- Learning about the different kinds of Indian embroideries.
- Becoming aware of the detailed process of embroidering.
- Appreciating the diversity of Indian embroidery and thread work.

How to do the activity:

- Students should study different styles of embroidery and learn how to do simple stitches.
- They can try their hand at various simple embroidery methods and designs.
- Students can then find out about the craftspersons specialising in this embroidery and chart the history of the embroidery and the family lineage of the craftspersons.

"The tiny needle, a flash of coloured thread, a peaceful silence – this is the ambience that envelops Indian embroiderers."
The Indian Crafts Journal, Dastkari Haat Samiti

WORLD EMBROIDERY DAY

World Embroidery Day is celebrated each year on 30th July. It was started by a group of eager embroiderers and it soon started getting celebrated in India. Many designers and craftspersons come together to promote Indian embroidery on this day.

DID YOU KNOW?

Gara is the Gujarati word for *saree* and the thread embroidery reflects the cultural heritage of three regions – Persia, China and India. *Gara* embroidered *sarees* are worn by Parsi ladies during special occasions and festivals.

The Simple Stitch

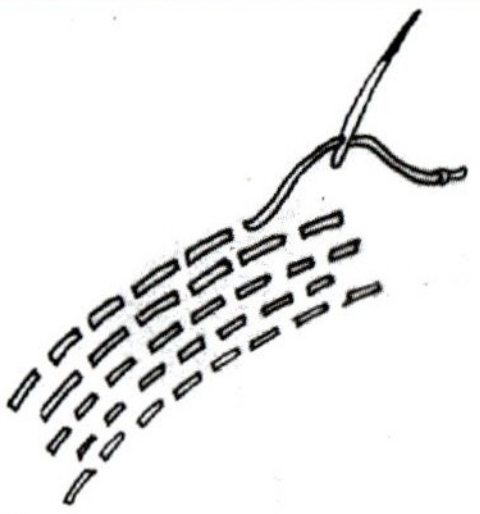

Try your hand at simple stitches such as a running stitch, chain stitch and satin stitch. Watch tutorials online and try and embroider something beautiful. Click a photograph of the same and paste it in the given box.

Embroidery Equivalent

Match the following

1. **Phulkari**
   An embroidery style from Punjab, characterised by geometric and floral designs which are made using untwisted floss silk threads.

2. **Kantha**
   The run stitch embroidery of Bengal, traditionally done by women on recycled old material or waste cloth.

3. **Chikankari**
   This is a white-on-white embroidery style. Floral patterns are stitched using untwisted white cotton/silk threads.

4. **Kutch Embroidery**
   Chain and open chain stitching is employed with abundant use of mirrors, beads, shells and colourful threads in this embroidery of the Kutch region of Gujarat.

5. **Kashida**
   This is an intricate needlework from Kashmir which is inspired by the daily surroundings and nature. Multi-coloured threads are used in this form.

6. **Kasuti**
   This is double-sided embroidery from Karnataka in which identical geometric patterns are stitched perfectly on either side of the cloth.

a. 

b. 

c. 

d. 

e. 

f. 

Step Ahead: Thread and Voice

Research on the role of craftspersons in Indian embroidery traditions and write down your observations. Have a discussion about the communities associated with this craft.

ACTIVITY 4

Enchanting Embellishments

Study the variety of textile embellishments

Educational goals:

- Learning about the different kinds of Indian embellishments.
- Understanding how complicated and remarkable the process of making embellishments is.
- Appreciating the beauty of the various kinds of textile embellishments.

How to do the activity:

- Students can study how to use different materials like wire, fabric pieces, and oil to embellish cloth.
- They can then make a beautiful fabric using simple appliqué techniques. The final fabrics can be showcased in the classroom.
- Students may research about the history and community involved with the craft. They can also make presentations on the craft and present it in class.

TEXTILE ORNAMENTATIONS

***Zardozi* embroidery**: The name is derived from *Zar* which means gold and *dozi* which means work. In this style, gold and silver threads and other semi precious embellishments are used for embroidery. It is practiced in parts of Uttar Pradesh, Delhi and Jaipur.

***Appliqué* work**: An elaborate needlework wherein fabric pieces are cut in different shapes and sizes and stitched on top of the base fabric. It is practiced in Pipli in Odisha, Rampur and Aligarh in Uttar Pradesh, and parts of Rajasthan and Bihar.

***Rogan* printing**: A type of cloth painting practiced in Nirona, Gujarat. Castor or sunflower oil is heated which produces a thick residue called *rogan* (paint) which is applied on cloth using a stylus.

DID YOU KNOW?

Wings of Buprestidae beetles were popularly used to embellish Indian fabrics in the 19th century. The wings were cut, shaped and stitched using a metal thread on the fabric.

Amazing Appliqué

Learn the technique

Learn the technique of appliqué with the following steps:

Step 1: Prepare the pieces of fabric; cut them into desired shapes i.e. geometric designs or flowers using scissors.

Step 2: Lay them on a big piece of base fabric in a desired manner and secure them with pins.

Step 3: Sew them with your teachers' or parents' help.

Step 4: Remove the secured pins as you progress until all the pieces are neatly sewed.

Step 5: The appliqué textile is ready! Paste a picture of your creation in your notebook.

Zardozi Karigar

Live the life!

Imagine you are a master *zardozi karigar*. Describe a day in your life and share how, using material and embellishments from your region, you have created a masterpiece.

Preserve, Protect and Promote

Write a letter to the local authorities to preserve, protect and promote the dying textile art of *rogan* painting. Use the given template for the letter and make useful suggestions to the local authorities.

Date:

Dear Sir,

I, ____________________________________

urge you to kindly protect the endangered art of *rogan* painting. This textile craft is only practiced by a family in Nirona, Gujarat. We would like to suggest the following ways in which *rogan* painting can be protected and promoted:

____

____

____

____

____

____

Thanking you,
Name of Student:
School:
City:

ACTIVITY 5

Intricate Kalamkari

Gain the knowledge of Kalamkari

Educational goals:

- Understanding the ways of painting textiles using pens.
- Learning about the detailed technique of preparing a *kalamkari* saree.
- Distinguishing between different types of *kalamkari* styles.

How to do the activity:

- Students can try their hands on the art of colouring with a pen.
- The teacher can then conduct a class group activity using cloth pieces on which students should draw motifs using pens. They can also colour these motifs.
- They should observe the process of preparing the fabric and learn the details of the process by viewing films on *kalamkari*.

KINDS OF KALAMKARI

The two popular styles of *kalamkari* art from Andhra Pradesh are – Srikalahasti and Machilipatnam style.

In the Machilipatnam style, motifs are printed with hand-carved traditional blocks and intricate detailing painted by the *kalam*. This style employs neutral and monotones in its *kalamkaris*.

The Srikalahasti style of painting draws inspiration from the Hindu mythology, describing scenes from the epics and folklore. All gods are showcased in bright blue, female characters in golden yellow and demons in red.

DID YOU KNOW?

The popular *kalamkari* motif of the Mother Goddess signifies creation, fertility, life, motherhood, and the earth.

Know the Kalamkari

Create this traditional design

Looking at the sample of the typical floral *kalamkari* design, make a similar one in your own way.

Kalamkari Katha

Following is the process of preparing the fabric of the *kalamkari* saree.

Cow Dung Bleach
Cow dung+water +buffalo milk
Stir and soak the fabric well
→ **Washing**
→ **Myrabolum treatment**
Myrabolum powder+water
→ **Sketching and colouring**
Drawing of motifs and filling them using natural colours
→ **Kalamkari**
Black liquid is used for the outline. Mordant (alum liquid) is used for filling colours
↓ **Running Water Washing**
← **Colour Development**
Boiling the fabric by gradually increasing the heat with the ingredients, alizarin and dye
← **Washing**
The fabric is washed over twenty times
← **Fixation**
Fabric is dipped and stirred in the alum water
← **Dry the fabric**

Find and research about the following keywords mentioned in the process of making a *kalamkari* saree.

Mordant____________________

Alum Liquid____________________

Myrabolum Powder____________________

Alizarin____________________

ACTIVITY 6

Painted Patterns

Dwell in the world of painted textiles

DID YOU KNOW?

The ancient technique of batik was revived in Santiniketan's Visvabharati University by Rabindranath Tagore after his visit to Java in Indonesia.

Educational goals:

- Recognising traditional ways of painting textiles.
- Discovering the range of material used to prepare such painted cloth.
- Learning the significance this painting has in textiles.

How to do the activity:

- Students can be made aware of the methods of decorating textiles.
- Teachers can help the students arrange an activity class where they make batik style fabrics.
- Using the steps mentioned they can make their own batik print cloth piece/t-shirt.

Beautiful Batik

Using the following instructions make your own batik print cloth.

Material Required:

Pencil and paper, cloth piece (or t-shirt or dupatta), scissors, old newspaper, fabric dyes, paint brushes, wax or glue, empty bottle for wax, double boiler (to melt the wax), gloves

Step 1: Children can draw any design on a piece of paper and trace it on a white cloth/t-shirt.

Step 2: With the help of an adult and using gloves, melt the wax in a double boiler. Either pour the wax in a bottle or use a paint brush to trace the drawing. (Glue can also be used instead of wax).

Step 3: Let the wax dry overnight and then put it into a tub filled with hot dye. You can even paint the cloth with fabric paints instead. Make sure you crack the wax a little to create the effect.

Step 4: Scrape off the wax with your hands or a dull knife.

Step 5: Wash the cloth after taking off the wax. Your batik is now ready!

Textile Stories

kapad katha

"In India, as in other civilisations,
weaving is considered as an act of creation and worship.
Many of the weaver communities...
believe that their progenitors were linked to the lord of creation..."

Jasleen Dhamija, *Sacred Textiles of India*

ACTIVITY 1

Woven Tales

Learn about stories depicted in textiles

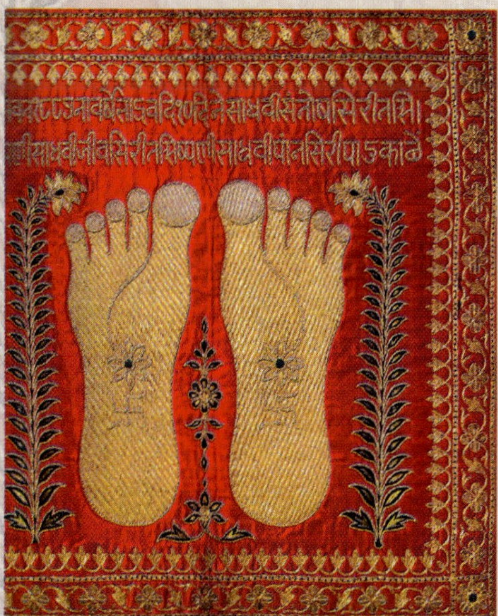

Educational goals:

- Understanding the unique cultural narratives that are woven in the fabric.
- Admiring the living heritage that is associated with textiles.

How to do the activity:

- Students can research on stories woven into textiles.
- Students can find family heirlooms which have a story depicted in them and bring those to class.
- An interesting storytelling session can then be done in the classroom.

DID YOU KNOW?

Balucharis had religious connotations and sometimes reflected nationalistic ideas. A saree in the Sanskriti Museum of Indian Textiles has the inscription of *Bande-Mataram* woven on the *pallu* and border.

TEXTILE TALES

Naga shawls of different kinds are worn by most groups in Nagaland. The Naga shawls distinctively uses a bright red and black colour palette and each shawl is embroidered with specific motifs. The embroidery signifies the philosophical understanding of the universe, derived from Naga cosmology.

WOVEN EXCELLENCE

Baluchari is a traditional woven silk saree that comes from Baluchar village in West Bengal. The traditional saree consists of floral or geometric silk brocade designs. The main theme depicts mythological stories and folk tales on the *pallus* of sarees.

Shawl Reflections

Study this bold Naga design

- What do you see in the shawl border above? Can you describe the theme?
- What are the dominant colours used here?
- Drawing inspiration from the motifs on the textile, make a border in a similar style.

Baluchari Tales

Study this detailed saree palla

- What figurative motifs do you see woven in the saree?
- Are the motifs connected to each other?
- Pick the most distinguishing motif and illustrate it innovatively.

ACTIVITY 2

Stitches Speak

Stitching makes colourful stories

Educational goals:

- Developing the skill of story interpretation by observation of motifs.
- Identifying the varieties of stitches used in textiles.
- Understanding how stitches have a story to tell.

How to do the activity:

- Students can study the different textiles and stories depicted in the designs.
- They can understand the symbolism of certain motifs and colours used.
- They can watch films on textiles which bring out a story and then share the story in class.

CHAMBA RUMAL

The Chamba *rumal* is a fine display of embroidery and crafts traditions. The most popular story appearing on the *rumal* is that of *Krishna* and the *gopis*. Other themes include stories from the *Bhagvat Purana*, *Mahabharata* and *Ramayana*. They were originally created by the ladies of the former court of Chamba to wrap royal wedding gifts.

DID YOU KNOW?

The embroidery found on a *phulkari* depicts various stories. For example, flower motifs signify marital bliss and blessings for a new bride, while trains found on some rare *phulkaris* show the story of the arrival of trains in rural Punjab.

Chart the Chamba

Observe this charming circular Chamba rumal

- What do you think is depicted in the embroidered *rumal*?
- What elements of the natural world can you see in the *rumal*?
- If you were a queen of Chamba today what design would you use for your Chamba *rumal*?

Exploring Embroidered Textiles

Watch *Tanko Bole Chhe*, an animated documentary by Kalaraksha Trust about the Kutch artisans (available on Youtube) and share similar stories.

You can also watch films about textiles on the Young INTACH YouTube Page – www.youtube.com/c/YOUNGINTACH

ACTIVITY 3

Painted Stories

Engage with scrolls

Pabuji ka Phad

Cheriyal Scroll Painting

Educational goals:

- Gaining knowledge about the oral narratives associated with cloth scrolls.
- Understanding the role of the artists involved in making the scroll and the storytelling aspects.
- Appreciating the heritage that is associated with these interesting scrolls.

How to do the activity:

- Encourage students to study the use of scrolls in storytelling.
- Students can research on local and regional storytelling traditions that exist and narrate the stories in class.
- They should study the different techniques used to make cloth scrolls.
- Based on their learning, students can further take up the role of storytellers and engage in a group activity of reciting songs related to the stories on scrolls.

STORIES ON CLOTH

Pabuji ka Phad

These are folk tales of Rajasthan that are painted on a cotton textile scroll. The legend of *Pabuji* and *Devnarayan* (local deity and hero) are painted on the scroll and recited by the *bhopa* (storyteller).

Cheriyal Scroll Painting

These are Telangana scroll paintings done on khadi cloth, made in Cheriyal town. They depict local stories and Indian mythologies in linear strips. Scenes from daily rural life are reflected too.

Pattachitra

Pattachitra of Odisha and West Bengal

These are traditional cloth-based scroll paintings that depict stories of Hindu deities. In the Bengal *pattachitra*, there is always a song associated with it that is sung by the *patuas* while unfurling the scroll.

Ponder over the Phad

Observe this colourful scroll

- Identify the character on the horse and write about his story?
- Observe the scroll painting and mention all the elements that you spot. For eg, *mandapa*, tiger, horse, tree, etc.
- What are the colours used in the *phad* ? Which is the most predominant colour and why?
- Pick your favourite character and try painting him/her in a similar style.
- Find out the community associated with the painting of these scrolls and write a short paragraph on these artists.
- Research on the *bhopas* or the bard community and their connection with these scrolls.
- Listen to a Pabuji ka Phad song, and create one in your native language based on this scroll painting. You can then sing the song in your class to narrate this story!

Picturesque Pattachitra

Study this Odisha *pattachitra*

- State the colours used in the *pattachitra* and their sources. (eg. limestone for white and turmeric for yellow)
- What are the different elements of flora depicted in the *pattachitra*?
- What do you see in the *pattachitra*? Write a story associated with the two main characters.

Evocative Imagery

Understand this Bengali *pattachitra*

- What story do you think is depicted in the *pattachitra*?
- What is the significance of this central figure?
- Find out about the storytellers who recite the story on these scrolls and share.
- Find out about the importance of the figure in Bengali culture and its UNESCO recognition.

ACTIVITY 4

Venerable Votives

Discover the world of votives

Educational goals:

- Learning about the stories depicted and values linked with them.
- Familiarising oneself with the significance of central figures in votive textiles.

How to do the activity:

- Students can research about the significance of votive central figures in sacred textiles.
- They can research and write down the religious and spiritual stories connected with votive textiles.
- They can bring a religious textile to class and explain its significance to their friends!

Thangka Painting

MATA NI PACHEDI

It is a cloth with the figure of the Mother Goddess which is mostly worshipped during the *Navratri* festival. Some of these cloths also include sacred figures and images from religious epics.

THANGKAS

Buddhist paintings on cloth that depict Buddha's life and teachings. *Thangkas* are originally created for meditation purposes and displayed in monasteries. *Thangkas* have multiple layers, are mounted on a brocaded textile and have a thin veil on top as well. They are created in the form of scrolls, are unframed, and are rolled up and kept away when not in use.

Pious Paintings

Observe this Mata ni Pachedi

- Identify the Mother Goddess in the textile. Find out why she is revered?
- List down all the elements that you see being depicted in the textile.
- Research and find out what this textile is used for too.

Mystical Thangkas

Study and admire this votive textile

- Identify the main character of the *thangka* painting.
- What is the primary colour used and how is it sourced/made?
- What is depicted around the central figure?
- Find out the relevance of the lotus on the base of the central figure in the painting.
- What are the various themes and scenes that are often depicted in *thangka* paintings?
- What is the importance of nature portrayed in *thangkas*?

Chadar Charms

Explore this revered covering

A *chadar* is an offering presented at dargahs around the country as a sign of respect for the saints buried there. They are made out of different types of cloth and are highly decorated.

- What kind of embellishments can you recognise on this *chadar*?
- What writing is generally embroidered on a *chadar* and what does it signify?
- *Chadars* are offered in many dargahs. Mention any four such sacred places.

1.____

2.____

3.____

4.____

Votive Veils

Appreciate the intricate artistry

- Identify the motifs used on this tabernacle (a locked box where the Holy Communion is stored before it is distributed) veil and research on their significance.
- What are the colours generally used in such sacred textiles in churches?

Apparel and Attire

Poshaak aur Pehnawa

*"Weaves, patterns, drapes, aesthetics and expressions...
this one garment (sari)
succinctly captures India's incredible diversity.
When you travel across the length and breadth of the country,
you will spot the humble sari being woven and worn in myriad ways,
each reflective of the region, its culture and textile heritage."*

Rta Kapur Chishti, *Saris: Tradition and Beyond*

ACTIVITY 1

Saree – India's Pride

Discover the beauty of the saree

Educational goals:

- Identifying the journey of the saree.
- Understanding the importance of the saree as India's representative attire.
- Learning the art of tying a saree.
- Recognising the creativity that is involved in the draping of a saree.

How to do the activity:

- Students can learn how to tie a saree from their family members or teachers.
- They can research on sarees worn in India and identify their significance.
- They can observe sarees and describe them in creative ways.
- The students can learn about their mother's or grandmother's or friends' favourite saree.

SAREE SAGA

The origin of the saree can be traced back to Ancient India and the Harappan Civilisation where it was worn as a single piece of cloth as unstitched cloth was considered pure.

In Medieval India sarees underwent a change. This included the introduction of a blouse-like covering, a *pallu* and distinctive borders in sarees.

With the advent of the Colonial period, petticoats and blouses were introduced. It is believed that Jnanadanandini Devi, wife of Rabindranath Tagore's brother, Satyendranath, popularised the modern style of wearing a saree with a blouse and petticoat.

My Saree Story

Write an essay on the saree. You can also include a description of your mother/ grandmother/ relative/ friend's favourite saree and why it is special for them.

____

____

____

____

____

DID YOU KNOW?

What is a saree?

A saree is a long and wide piece of cloth worn by women in the Indian subcontinent as a garment. The most common style worn today is known as the **Nivi drape**.

Praiseworthy Saree

A cinquain is a five line poem consisting of 10 words. The first line is a word (noun), second line is two words (adjectives), the third line is three words (verbs), the fourth is feeling words and the fifth is one word (synonym).

Observe the cinquain on cotton below and write another one of your own on the saree.

Cotton	Saree
Soft Airy	_______________
Spinning Weaving Dyeing	_______________
Awe Appreciate Care Cherish	_______________
Cloth	_______________

Fun with Drapes

Make an interesting sketch of an Indian woman wearing a saree and a blouse with unique motifs and borders.

ACTIVITY 2

Saree Spread

Learn about the regional variations of sarees

Educational goals:

- Identifying regional draping styles from various parts of India.
- Understanding styles and their history.
- Exploring regional as well as tribal sarees and their significance.
- Learning about the functionality of various saree drapes.

How to do the activity:

- Students can find out about the different draping styles used in India.
- Students must research on the origins and functionality of different drapes.
- They can find out similarities and differences across different regions including tribal sarees.
- Students can style different saree drapes belonging to different parts of the country and have a saree show in school.

DID YOU KNOW?

The Ilkal saree is typically woven within a family. A father-daughter or husband-wife team weave the *pallu* together, making it a collective process.

WONDERFUL VARIATIONS

Sarees in India are draped in numerous ways, depending on their history. Saree drapes often vary with the occupation of the person wearing it and the local customs. They also change with festivals and occasions.

WORLD SAREE DAY

The 21st of December is celebrated every year as World Saree Day to honour the elegance and beauty of this ancient drape!

Wearing a Saree in Simple Steps

Southern Sarees

Observe as well as research about the Southern sarees and then bring out the differences in their drapes. Some examples are given below.

Nambudiri

The traditional saree of Kerala is made of two *veshtis* of 2 yards each and draped with two pieces of white cloth, usually with gold brocade *pallus* and borders.

Pinkosu

This Tamilian nine-yard saree's tying style dates back to 2nd century BCE. The lower half of the saree is draped like a *dhoti* and the upper half is draped with pleats like a traditional saree.

Coorgi

Popular in Karnataka, the pleats are tucked at the back of the waist and the end of the saree is taken below the left shoulder. It is then secured over the right shoulder in a knot called '*molakattu*'.

Tribal Drapes

Tribal sarees are draped according to functionality, by women inhabiting different terrains. Research about the given tribal sarees and fill in the details including region, wearing styles and colours of the saree.

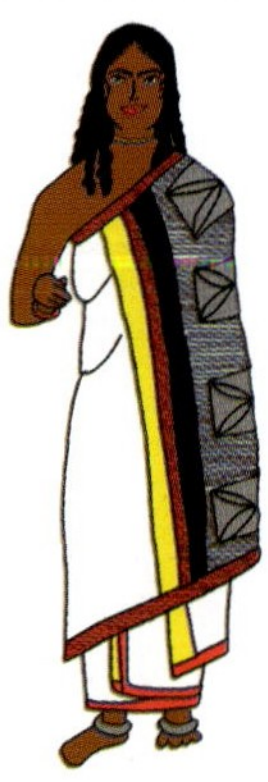

Toda

____

____

____

____

Santhal

____

____

____

____

Irula

____

____

____

____

Western Wonders

Sarees in Gujarat, Rajasthan, Maharashtra and Goa, have their own unique styles of draping. These styles are dependent on communities, cultural influences and varied landscapes.

DID YOU KNOW?

The Surguja drape is worn by the rural communities of Chhattisgarh.

Marwadi Saree

The most famous traditional western saree is the Marwadi saree worn by women in Maharashtra and Rajasthan. The lower part is worn like a *dhoti* and upper half is worn like a nivi drape.

Gujarati Saree

The Gujarati saree or *seedha pallu* is draped in an anticlockwise direction. After draping, the *pallu* is pulled from the rear to the front on the right shoulder, tucking its free-end into the left waist.

Goan Saree

Typically worn by the Kunbi and Gawda tribes of Goa, this short saree was made for the ease of working in paddy fields. It is draped by tying in the fabric below the shoulder and a strip of saree is crossed over the left shoulder.

Recreate the Style

Students can recreate the style of Raja Ravi Varma's paintings and paste the photographs of their recreated look and the painting chosen in a notebook.

NAUVARI SAREE

The nine yard long saree is worn without a petticoat by Maharashtrian women. This *dhoti* style saree also suited women warriors.

Novel North-East and East

- In Assam, a unique saree is made up of two parts, the *Mekhla* and the *Chador*.
- The *Moirang Phee* saree of Manipur worn by the Metei community is made from fine cotton and now includes designs such as animals, flowers, leaves, etc.
- The traditional Bengali saree comes in a white colour and has a red border. It is draped in the *Atpoure* style with box pleats in the front.

Mekhla Chador

Moirang Phee

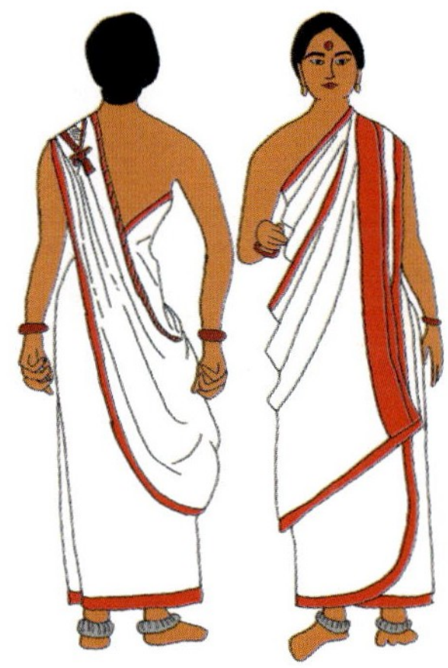

Atpoure

Saree Show

Have a saree day in school with each student draping a saree in different ways. Paste a photograph of yourself and your friends wearing sarees in various drape styles.

Read and Learn More!

- *Saris of India: Tradition and Beyond* by Rta Kapur Chishti
- *Saris: An Illustrated Guide to the Indian Art of Draping* by Chantal Boulanger
- *The Sari* by Linda Lynton
- *Sarees of India* by Nanda Nandan Mahapatra

ACTIVITY 3

Diverse Dresses

Begin a dress journey across India

Veshti Mundu

Dhoti Kurta

Educational goals:

- Learning about different Indian dresses.
- Understanding how Indian dresses are identity markers for people and communities.
- Appreciating the diversity of Indian costumes and their intricate designs.

How to do the activity:

- Students may find out about the unique Indian dresses.
- They can make interesting cards using different costumes.

DRESS – DOWN THE AGES

Indian costumes have been a visual identifier of people for centuries. Some popular Indian costumes are:

Veshti Mundu: *Veshtis* and *mundus* are worn in Kerala and Tamil Nadu. Men wear the *mundu* wrapped around the waist, while women wear the set-*mundu*.

Dhoti Kurta: *Dhoti* is an unstitched piece of cloth which is wrapped around the waist with twists around the ankle. It is sometimes accompanied by a *kurta*.

India's Diverse Dresses

Ensemble Excursion

Ghaghara Choli

Ghaghara is a long skirt worn with a tight fitted blouse called *choli* and an *odhani*, which is a light cover or *dupatta.*

Churidar Kurta

Churidar is worn by both men and women over a *kurta.* They are narrow fitted pants that are longer than the leg. The excess length falls into folds and appears like bangles.

Salwar Kameez

The traditional outfit comprises of *salwar*, which is a loose-fitting trouser with narrow hems at the end and a tunic called the *kameez.* It is commonly worn by women in North India.

Mekhala and Kilt

The Angami Naga men wear kilts and wrappers with a white cotton cloth tied around the waist. Females wear a skirt, shawl and an apron which rolls down to the knees.

Sharara

This is a flared trouser joined around the knee level. It is part of a three-piece dress with a short tunic and a *dupatta.*

Sherwani

It is a long-sleeved coat worn by men on special occasions over pyjamas or *churidars.*

Know-the-Costume Card

Make a Know-the-Costume card on the costumes of your region with the following information.

Name of the costume ____________________

Who wears it ____________________

Two distinct features____________________

ACTIVITY 4

Assorted Accessories

Enter the world of headgears and accessories

Educational goals:

- Recognising the use of local textiles in making headgear and accessories.
- Identifying the regional variations of headgear and accessories.
- Understanding their significance for the communities.

How to do the activity:

- Students can conduct a study of their region's textile accessories.
- They can research and identify the headgear and match it with its characteristics.
- Students can also discuss the various kinds of headgears and accessories they see around them on their travels or in their city.

DID YOU KNOW?

Paranda or *Parandi* is a traditional hair accessory from Punjab, made from fabric threads.

FROM HEAD TO TOE

Headgear: Headgear is worn by both men and women for numerous purposes which include - climate, community, religion, status, etc. Some of the headgears worn in India are *puneri* turban, *dastar*, *perak*, mysore *peta*, *hijab*, *karakul* cap, etc.

***Dupattas* or Scarves:** Traditional Indian *dupattas* or scarves are common in an Indian woman's cupboard. They are made of different fabrics and can be decorated using a variety of adornments.

Scarf

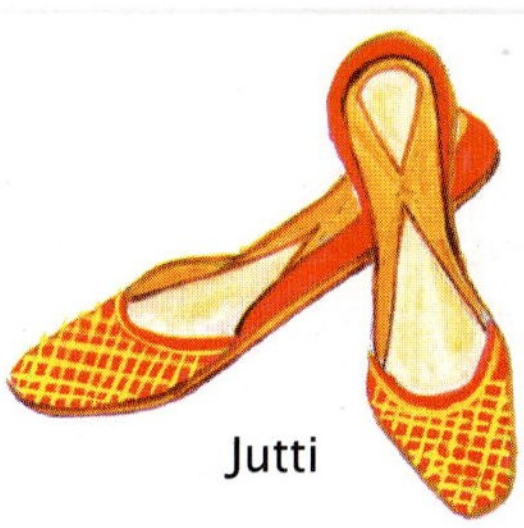

Jutti

Footwear: The *jutti* is a common footwear in North India and neighbouring regions. They are traditionally made of leather, covered with cloth and then decorated with intricate thread embroidery.

Woollen shoes such as the *thigme pabu* are popular in regions like Ladakh. These are expertly designed and beautifully decorated with embroidery.

Thigme pabu

Colourful Crowns

Uncover the mystery of India's headgears!

The assortment of headgears and accessories found in India is an apt representation of the country's rich diversity. Match the picture cards with their corresponding information in the card game below. You may even cut out the cards and play this game with your friends!

A 	**1. DASTAR** Dastar is an important part of the Sikh identity. It is used to cover the long, uncut hair of Sikhs.	B 	**2. PUNERI TURBAN** The puneri turban is a symbol of pride and honour in the city of Pune since the 17th century.
3. KARAKUL CAP Also called the Kashmiri cap, this is worn on special occasions and as a symbol of honour.	C 	**4. HARYANVI TURBAN** Called khindka in the local language, it is worn during cultural dances and ceremonies.	D 
E 	**5. RAJASTHANI TURBAN** Also called a pagdi or safa, this brightly coloured headgear denotes status.	F 	**6. MYSORE PETA** Originally worn by the royal Wodeyars, this headgear is presented to dignitaries.
7. GUJARATI TURBAN A large and loosely rolled bright turban; this is also called phento.	G 	**8. HIMACHALI CAP** A grey or brown cap with a band of brightly coloured woven fabric.	H 

Stamp Collection

The Government of India released a series of 16 stamps in 2017 to commemorate the headgears of India, which are worn with great honour and pride across the country. You can find and collect at least 10 of these stamps in your notebook!

DID YOU KNOW?

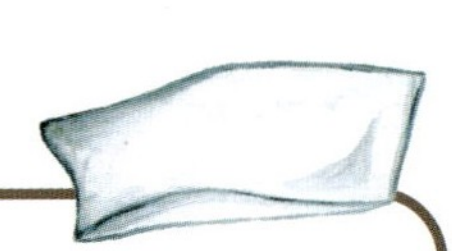

The Gandhi cap is a white cap made of khadi, pointed at both ends and having a wide band. Gandhiji popularised its use during the Indian Independence movement.

Kullu shawl

ACTIVITY 5

Splendid Shawls

Discover the world of Indian shawls

Educational goals:

- Promoting better understanding of a diverse range of shawls.
- Comprehending different patterns, designs and materials used in shawls across India.
- Recognising the diverse variety of indigenous shawls, both in cotton and wool.

How to do the activity:

- Students are divided into small groups and are asked to bring different kinds of shawls.
- They can do a sample study of different patterns, design and style of shawls.
- Students can look at the shawl designs and replicate the same.

Kashmiri shawl

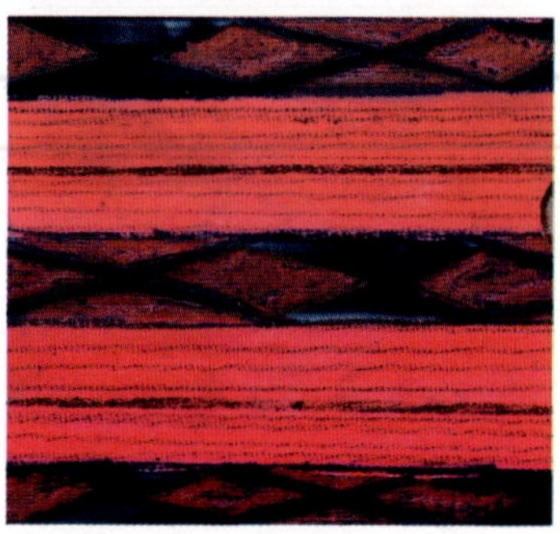

Chakhesang shawl

SHAWL STUDY

Shawls are rectangular pieces of cloth made of wool and cotton that have been around since ancient times.

Kashmiri Shawls: Traditionally made of shahtoosh or pashmina, Kashmiri shawls are known for their warmth, light weight and characteristic buta designs which include intricate hand embroidery techniques called *aari*, *kani*, and *sozni*.

Kullu Shawls: Also called *Loi*, Kullu shawls of Himachal are made with the wool of the Angora goat or local sheep. These shawls are distinguished by their striking motifs.

Chakhesang Shawls: The shawls of Nagaland are known for their unique colour palette of black and red.

Shawls in Style

Collect and paste photographs of different shawls from India and observe their design, style and pattern.

DID YOU KNOW?

During the 15th century, weaving of tapestry shawls was introduced from Turkistan by the ruler of Kashmir, Zain-ul-Abidin.

Shawl Sketching

Looking at the shawl designs below make similar ones in the given spaces.

DID YOU KNOW?

Himroo shawls of Aurangabad are made from silk and cotton threads. They are a reinterpretation of the Persian weave *Kinkhwab* which was meant for royalty.

Jhola Journey

Delve into the sustainable world of cloth bags!

Cloth bags have been made and used in India for centuries. They are made in many colours and weaves, and are replete with embroidery. The Rajasthani *jhola* and North-eastern striped bags are the most common cloth bags in India. They not only add colour to ones outfit, but are an integral part of a traditional costume.

With the world trying to reduce waste and be sustainable, cloth bags are in high demand not only in India, but all across the globe.

Try making a cloth bag yourself using the following steps:

1. Cut a rectangle of 32 inches x 24 inches out of leftover fabric or an old t-shirt, depending on the size you want.
2. Fold the cloth in half (16 inches x 12 inches) and then fold one of the long edges down by 4 inches (10 cm) and iron it with the help of an adult.
3. Repeat on the other side as well and sew across both the folded edges.
4. Turn the bag inside out.
5. To make a handle, cut two long strips of the same fabric and sew them on to the top of the bag.
6. You can decorate your bag with fabric paint, embroidery, sequins, or pieces of fabric.

Your cloth bag is now ready!

Joyful Jewellery

Learn about the innovative use of textile in jewellery

Textile jewellery has been worn over centuries in India to accessorise both men and women. Evidence of this has been found in Harappan sites. With the need to be more sustainable, fabric jewellery has increasingly become popular in modern times.

Create your own textile bracelet by taking three strands of leftover fabric (from an old t-shirt or *kurta*) and braiding them together. You can even choose fabrics of three different kinds to make this a colourful bracelet!

Craftsperson Speaks
karigar ki kahani

*"The act brings together threads into the magic of fabric.
Weaving our protective cover
showers honour on one who weaves.
Every other profession pales in comparison!"*

Late Chiluveru Ramalingam, weaver from Pochampalli, Telangana

ACTIVITY 1

Creative Craftspersons

Recognise the vital role of a craftsperson

"The lives of my family hang on the thread I embroider."
Ramba Ben, Embroiderer from Banaskantha, Gujarat

Educational goals:

- Finding out the role of different organisations in aiding and awarding craftspersons.
- Learning about the craftsperson and understanding their role in making textiles.
- Appreciating the efforts of the craftspersons and supporting their craft.

How to do the activity:

- Students can document a craftsperson's social and economic conditions.
- They can interview a local craftsperson engaged with any textile craft of their region and note down their observations.
- Students can make a field visit to a craft community/ cluster and engage with them as well as do a video documentation.

SUCCESS STORIES

Indian handloom industry is one of the largest economy generators in the country. Different handlooms have received government aid since Independence. One such textile craft that has received special support is Banarasi weaving.

Banarasi weavers have received tremendous support from the Uttar Pradesh Weavers Association. Many Government schemes have helped revive this beautiful textile craft.

KUTCHI CRAFT

Women of the Kutch region, Gujarat are known for their embroidery skills. One such community is the *Ahir* community whose embroidery is known for its use of mirrors and floral designs. Women often gather around their central courtyards and embroider together.

Artisan Testaments

Document the social and economic conditions of any craftsperson.

Interview a craftsperson living in your locality and ask them these questions.

Name of the Craftsperson:____________________

Community:____________________

How many generations are working on this textile craft?____________________

Has there has been a change in your social and economic condition? Are your children associated with this craft?

Are there any alternative sources of income?

Are you affiliated with any crafts organisation or council? If yes, which one?

Does the Government and/or NGOs help you? If yes, how?

Appreciate the Artisan

The craftsperson is responsible for creating textiles that portray Indian culture along with preserving this rich textile heritage for future generations. The tradition and skills of creating textiles are passed on through craftspersons.

Give three more reasons for recognising and appreciating our textile craftspersons.

Craft Cinema

Make a short film on a craftsperson on the theme 'A Day in the Life of a Craftsperson'.

ACTIVITY 2

Empowering Crafts

Learn about organisations that protect textiles

"[Muslin]...it was spun from our breath and woven in our hearts."
Jasleen Dhamija

Educational goals:

- Knowing about various organisations working for artisans, in handlooms and handicrafts.
- Understanding their role in artisan upliftment and revival of textile traditions.
- Appreciating and being inspired by pioneers who have led these organisations.

How to do the activity:

- Students can research on local/regional level organisations, self-help groups and centres that are working with textile makers.
- They can find out about the inception of certain craft organisations led by a pioneer and discuss in the classroom.
- They can visit the centres or bazaars and *haats* where they are representing their artisans' work and have a conversation about their work and future projects.

WE CARE FOR OUR TEXTILES!

National Textile Corporation (NTC) which was established in 1968 under the Ministry of Textiles, manages numerous textile mills for their proper running. It supports the textile industry and ensures the survival of textile businesses and traditions.

Jute Corporation of India Ltd. (JCI) was set up in 1971 to strengthen the jute industry. It does this by protecting the interest of jute farmers. This body works under the ambit of the Ministry of Textiles.

Self-Employed Women's Association (SEWA) is India's largest informal women's workers movement which was started before Independence. It provides employment to women in the production and marketing of textiles.

Dastkar established in 1981, this NGO works on uplifting and supporting local traditional craftspeople. Along with giving craftspeople economic opportunities and aid, Dastkar also ensures the survival of Indian textiles and handicrafts.

Exploring a Craft Bazaar

Visit one of the local craft *mela*, bazaar or *haat* and find out which organisation or self-help group the artisans are associated with. Write down your observations below:

Pioneer's Profile

Write a profile on any one pioneer who has started a craft organisation/group/centre working with textiles.

Pupul Jayakar

Logo Logic

Insert illustrations of logos of your local voluntary organisations working with textiles.

Write two lines in your notebook on each of your selected organisations.

1

2

ACTIVITY 3

Care and Conservation

Understand how textiles are cared for

Educational goals:

- Recognising the threats to textiles.
- Studying the various steps involved in textile conservation.
- Learning how to look after our personal textiles at home.
- Appreciating family textile heirlooms and their delicate conditions.

How to do the activity:

- Students can research and note down how they can protect their personal textiles.
- Students should choose a family textile heirloom and make its report.
- They can speak to an older family member to understand how textiles are valued and protected at home.
- Students can also visit a conservation laboratory nearby and watch how textiles are conserved by experts.

Causes of Textile Damage and Deterioration

- Light and Heat
- Temperature and Humidity
- Pollution
- Improper Display and Storage
- Damage due to Microorganisms and Insects

INTACH Conservation Institute (ICI)

The INTACH Conservation Institute Centre in Delhi is involved with the conservation of numerous textiles. The textile conservators provide stabilisation and support to the textiles, and minimise its further deterioration.

Steps of Textile Conservation

Examination – Preservation – Conservation – Cleaning – Flattening – Stabilisation

My Family Heirloom

Choose a textile that has been in your family for more than a decade and write down your relevant observations.

Textile (eg: *Patola, Ikat*):____________________

Where is it from?____________________

Kind of textile (silk, cotton, etc.)____________________

Age:____________________

What condition is the textile in currently?____________________

Do you think it requires some kind of conservation? If yes, what would you recommend?

Saree Speaks

Write your dialogue with an old silk saree in your family which was lovingly handed down the generations. The saree talks to you on how she sees different generations take her as a gift.

Saree:____________________

You:____________________

Saree:____________________

You:____________________

Saree:____________________

You:____________________

Tips to Take Care

- Wrap your precious heirloom in a soft cotton cloth.
- Put dried leaves of neem to prevent cloth from being eaten by moths.
- Always keep your silk clothes away from water as moisture can cause stains on to the fabric.
- Regularily change the folds of the saree or stole as folding on the same crease weakens the fibre of the cloth.

Home Care

Taking Care of Home Furnishings

Carpets and rugs are made of wool, silk or a blend of both and have intricate designs.

Durries are thin flat carpets used as floor coverings. Their size varies according to the function.

Home furnishings also include textiles such as curtains, upholstery, cushions, decorative pieces like torans, table linen, etc.

DID YOU KNOW?

A toran is hung above the doorway of the main entrance of a house as a sign of welcome. It is generally made of coloured cloth.

Do's

- ✓ Follow a proper cleaning routine so that dust and dirt are removed on time.
- ✓ Check for wear and tear and get repair work done.
- ✓ Use scissors to cut snags or threads from the carpet as it will improve the carpet's appearance and age.

Don'ts

- × Do not wash carpets at home using bleach or washing detergents.
- × Do not scrub the spilled stains as it will break the fibres of the delicate textiles.
- × Do not use all-purpose cleaning sprays.
- × Avoid touching cushions or sofas with wet and oily hands.

Modernisation and Machinery

adhunikta aur yantra

"Beginning in the seventeenth century,
Indian cottons, in fact,
were...the first global consumer commodity."

Sven Beckert, *Empire of Cotton: A Global History*

ACTIVITY 1

Modern Mills

Study the modernisation of Indian textiles

Educational goals:

- Learning about the history behind modern textile mills and machinery.
- Identifying what is required to set up a mill.
- Discovering textile mill centres in India.

How to do the activity:

- Students should research on the factors needed to set up mills.
- They can locate the mills found in different parts of India.
- Students should research on traditional and modern mills and discuss the pros and cons of each.

FROM MILLS TO TRADE

A large part of India's population has always been involved in the textile industry, in one way or another. Therefore, it is a vital part of India's economy and trade.

The setting up of textile mills in the 19th century helped modernise our textile industry. This increased its capacity but negatively impacted the handloom industry.

DID YOU KNOW?

A cotton mill at Fort Gloster near Kolkata (1818) was the first textile mill established in India. The Bombay Spinning and Weaving Company (1854) was the first successful mill in India.

Tata Empress Mill in Nagpur in 1877

Factor Study

Identify and understand the factors required to set up a cotton mill. Create a similar chart for a mill set up in your own region!

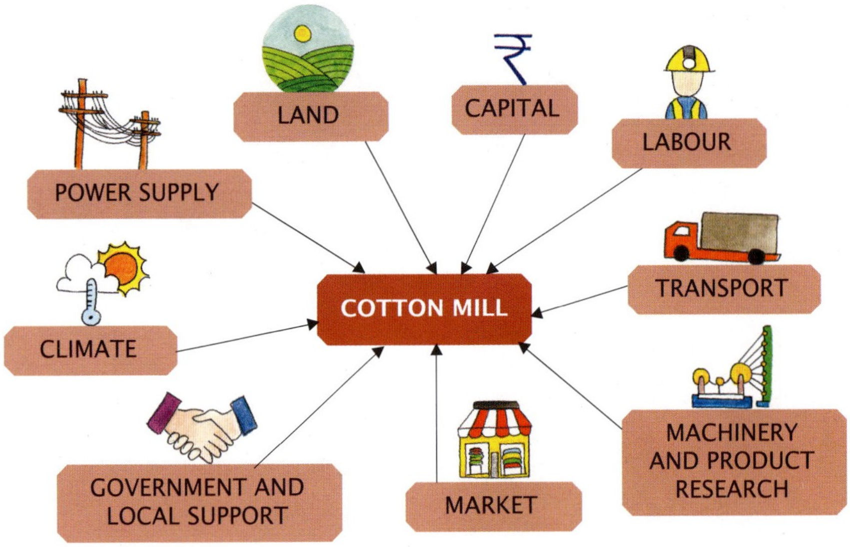

Locate the Textile Mills

Mark 10 textile mills in at least 5 States of India in the map given.

Textile Mills	State
1.	
2.	
3.	
4.	
5.	
6.	
7.	
8.	
9.	
10.	

Dynamic Discussion

Have a debate on the modern and traditional ways of textile production. Which method is better and why? Mention the pros and cons of each method. You should also discuss the concept of micro mills and power looms.

Sick Mill Study

A sick mill is one which is impacted adversely by a number of factors such as rising costs and outdated machinery. Study sick mills in India and how they are being revived by the government.

ACTIVITY 2

Contemporary Cloth

Trace the process of textile manufacture

Educational goals:

- Identifying and learning about textile machinery.
- Understanding how fabrics are processed and created in modern mills.
- Discovering new blended and synthetic textiles and their sources.

How to do the activity:

- Students should learn about the production of textiles in modern mills.
- They can study and write down the production chain of textiles.
- Students should visit a local market and get samples of synthetic and blended fabrics.
- They can then research on modern fabrics.

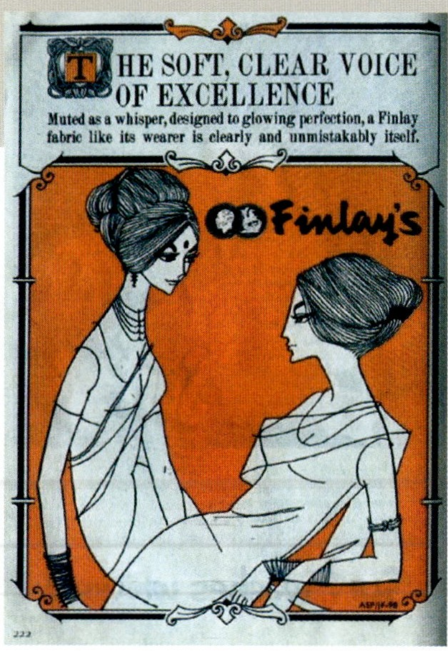

MODERN MACHINES

The spinning jenny was invented by James Hargreaves in 1764 in Lancashire, England. This machine modernised the cotton industry to a great extent by reducing the number of hours required to manufacture cotton, thereby increasing productivity.

Cotton to Cloth

Study the flow chart of how cotton is produced in mills and explain each process in the lines given.

COTTON PICKING

After plucking, cotton is removed from the vegetable matter through a picker.

GINNING AND BALING

Ginning is the process which is used to separate cottonseed from fiber which separates seeds and removes the impurities.

CARDING

After the cotton comes off of the picking machine in laps, it is then taken to carding machines. In this process, the fibres are separated and then assembled into a loose strand.

DRAWING, COMBING, ROVING

In Drawing the fibres are straightened with the help of a Drawing frame. Combing is optional, but is used to remove the shorter fibres to create a stronger yarn. In Roving frames, the yarn is made into a finer thread, giving it more twist and is more regular.

SPINNING

Spinning involves process of prepared cotton roving into workable yarn or thread.

A spinning jenny, originally invented by James Hargreaves

WEAVING AND FINISHING

The weaving process uses a loom. In the loom, it contains impurities and therefore requires further treatment to develop it into full textile.

DYEING AND PRINTING

At this stage, cotton is ready for colouration process and now printing is possible on dyed fabric which is the application of colour to the surface of a fabric.

Blended Fibres

Visit your local textile market and purchase samples of synthetic and blended fabrics. Bring them to class and share them with their names.

ACTIVITY 3

Textile Travels

Explore the journey of textile trade

DID YOU KNOW?

During the Sangam Age, when Romans came to India for trade, Poduke, known as Arikamedu (in present day Puducherry) was an important trading centre for textiles.

Educational goals:

- Learning the journey of textile and textile trade from India.
- Recognising the role of India's textile trade in the international market.
- Acquiring interpretation skills by the study of textile trade.

How to do the activity:

- Students learn about the importance of the ancient Silk Route.
- They can research on the recent trends of textile industry by a graphical study.
- They can learn about Indian exports and the role of various fabrics.

The Silk Road is the longest and most fascinating trade route connecting diverse cultures of Asia, Europe and Africa over centuries. Textiles travelled on this route and so did their techniques, varieties and ways of draping.

Sutra Journey

The technique of silk reeling came to India from China during the Gupta Period along the Silk Route.

Mesmerising Mulmul

It is believed that muslin was one of the main exports from the port of Machilipatnam in Andhra Pradesh, which the Romans called Maisolos.

THE SILK ROUTE

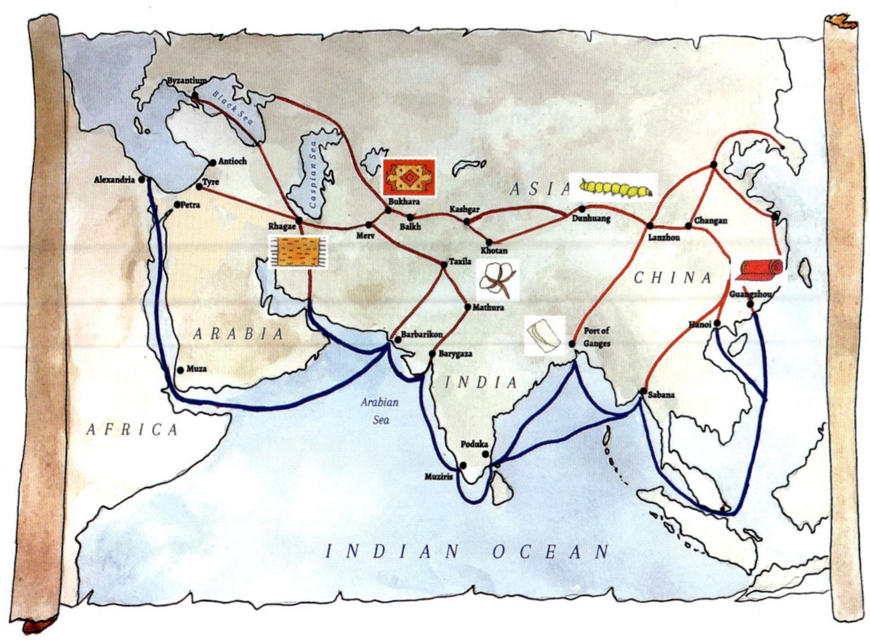

Yesterday, Today, Tomorrow...

Trading Timeline

Indian textiles had been known both for their fine quality and exquisite craftsmanship. They were extensively traded in Southeast Asia. European traders first encountered fine cotton cloth from India carried by Arab merchants in Mosul in present-day Iraq. In the 17th century, indiennes (printed and painted cotton fabrics from India) became a popular commodity in Europe.

Complete the timeline below mentioning the textiles traded with their origins and destinations:

Ancient	Mauryas	Gupta	Chola
Medieval	Mughals	Marathas	Vijayanagar
Modern	British	Portuguese	Post Independence

Textile Trade Today

Study the graphs given and answer the following questions:

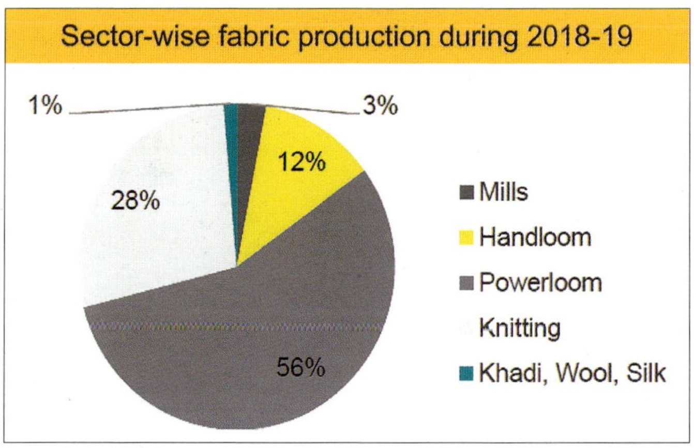

1. Which kind of fabric today accounts for the highest percentage? What is the percentage of mill-made fabric?
2. Can you find out why khadi, wool and silk contributes the least in the production?

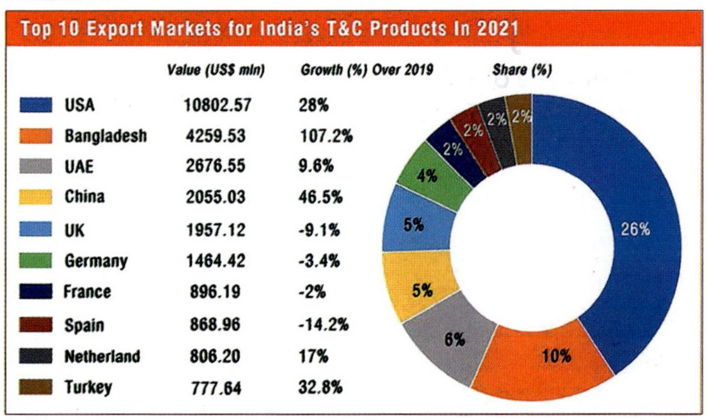

1. Find out the country which dominates India's export market in terms of the value.
2. Name the country which accounts for the maximum growth from 2019 to 2021?
3. Tabulate the share of the 10 countries in percentage in the given graph.

ACTIVITY 4

India Goes Global

Witness Indian textiles' worldwide reach

Educational goals:

- Discovering the impact of Indian textiles in the world.
- Learning about the innovative use of different plants to make fibres.
- Appreciating the use of sustainable fibres in today's fashion.

How to do the activity:

- Students can research on how global fashion is being influenced by Indian designers and textiles.
- They may design and draw their own modern dress with the use of traditional elements.
- Students should make a presentation on sustainable and unique fibres being used today.

DID YOU KNOW?

Sustainable clothing uses biodegradable components from natural or recycled fibres. Some weavers in India use fibres of pineapple and banana to make sarees. The fibre is extracted from the leaves of the pineapple and the trunk of the banana tree. There are references of banana fibre being used in ancient India to weave sarees.

FASHIONING THE CONTEMPORARY

Multiple contemporary designers, both in India and abroad, have adopted Indian styles, designs, and fabrics in their collections to evoke the vision of exquisitely embroidered and printed garments. Some of the globally favoured Indian fabrics include muslin, velvet, *zardozi*, brocade, and *chikankari*.

Modern Mastery

Draw a modern outfit using traditional Indian textiles and styles and label your outfit. Then write a line or two on each element as well.

Local to Global

Research and write about a fashion designer who has taken Indian textiles and fashion forward to the global stage.

Fibre to Fashion

Innovative and sustainable materials are being used to make fibres and textiles in recent times. For example, lotus fibre or silk is derived from the stem and is used to create clothing and other home textiles.

Choose any one other unique fibre such as bamboo, banana, rose, etc. Make a presentation on it and show it in class.

Lotus Silk

TEXTILE MUSEUMS

Anokhi Museum, Jaipur

Assam State Museum, Guwahati

Jawaharlal Nehru State Museum, Itanagar

Kasturi Srinivasan Art Gallery and Textile Museum, Coimbatore

Living and Learning Design Centre, Bhuj

Manipur State Museum, Imphal

Meghalaya State Museum, Shillong

Mizoram State Museum, Aizawl

Moda Goa Museum and Research Centre, Colvale, Goa

Mumbai Mill Museum, Indian United Mills, Mumbai

National Handicrafts and Handlooms Museum, Delhi

National Museum, Delhi

Salar Jung Museum, Hyderabad

Sanskriti Museum of Indian Textiles, Delhi

Textile Museum of Ladakh, Leh

The Calico Museum of Textiles, Ahmedabad

Tribal Museum, Delhi

Tripura Government Museum, Agartala

Victoria Memorial Hall, Kolkata

Vimor Museum of Living Textiles, Bengaluru

GLOSSARY:

Alizarin: A red pigment derived from the madder root used for dyeing.

Batik: A cloth dyed using wax and dyes to create unique patterns.

Brocade: This is a silk fabric with rich patterns in gold and silver.

Charkha: It is a domestic spinning wheel generally used to spin cotton.

Gopura: A large tower placed upon the entry gate of a temple precinct.

Haat: This is a local open-air market with traditional handicrafts.

Handloom: A manually operated loom to weave cloth from threads.

Ikat: A unique fabric where the fibres are dyed before weaving.

Jhola: A traditional satchel or cloth bag.

Kalamkari: This is a cotton cloth in which designs are printed by hand.

Karigar: An artisan, generally creating traditional items.

Khadi: An Indian homespun cotton cloth.

Khesh: A kind of Bengali weaving using old cotton sarees.

Mechanical loom: This is a mechanised loom operated with electricity.

Mulmul: A thin lightweight cotton fabric.

Muslin: A lightweight fine cotton cloth.

Palanquin: This is a covered structured for one passenger which is carried on two horizontal poles.

Pallu: The loose end of a saree, which is often replete with designs.

Rumal: A handkerchief.

Shuttle: It is a spool with **two pointed ends used for carrying threads during weaving.**

Sutra: The traditional name for a thread.

Warp and Weft: The two components used to weave thread into fabric.

Zardozi: This is metal embroidery that is done with gold or silver threads.

Zari: The thread made of gold or silver.

SECTION DIVIDERS:

Hindi	**English**
tanna banna (ताना बाना)	Warp and Weft
kalam kashida (कलम कशीदा)	Pen and Embroidery
kapad katha (कापड़ कथा)	Textile Stories
poshaak aur pehnawa (पोशाक और पहनावा)	Apparel and Attire
karigar ki kahani (कारीगर की कहानी)	Craftsperson's Story
adhunikta aur yantra (आधुनकि्ता और यन्त्र)	Modernity and Machinery

BIBLIOGRAPHY

PUBLICATIONS:

Agrawal, Yashodhara: *Silk Brocades*, 2003, Lustre

Beckert, Sven: *Empire of Cotton: A New History of Global Capitalism*, 2015, Penguin

Bhandari, Vandana: *Textiles and Crafts of India*, 1998, Prakash Book Depot

Boulanger, Chantal: *Saris: An Illustrated Guide to the Indian Art of Draping*, 1997, Shakti Pr

Bühler, Alfred: 'Indian Resist-dye Fabrics', *Treasures of Indian Textiles,* 1980

Chisti, Rta Kapur: *Saris: Tradition and Beyond*, 2013, Lustre

Dhamija, Jasleen: *Handwoven Fabrics of India*, 1989

Dhamija, Jasleen: *Sacred Textiles of India*, 2014, The Marg Foundation

Edwards, Eiluned: *Block Printed Textiles of India: Imprints of Culture*, 2016, Niyogi Books

Gillow, John: *Indian Textiles*, 2014, Thames and Hudson Ltd

Gillow, John and Nicholas Barnard, *Traditional Indian Textiles*, 1993, Thames and Hudson Ltd

IGNCA, *Resurgence: Revival of Indian Embroideries*, 2013, Aryan Books International

Irwin, John and Margaret Hall: *Indian Painted and Printed Fabrics,* 1971, The Calico Museum of Textiles

Jain, Rahul: *Rapture: The Art of Indian Textiles*, 2011, Niyogi Books

Jayakar, Pupul: 'Indian Fabrics in Indian Life', *Textiles and Ornaments of India,* 1956, Museum of Modern Art

Krishna, Anand and Vijay Krishna: *Banaras Brocades,* 1966, Crafts Museum

Murphy, Veronica and Rosemary Crill: *Tie-Dyed Textiles of India (Victoria and Albert Museum-Indian Art Series)*, 1991, Rizzoli

National Institute of Fashion Technology, *Textiles and Crafts of India*, 1998, Prakash Book Depot

Oberoi, Bindu: *The Textile Industry In India: Changing Trends and Employment Challenges*, 2016, Oxford University Press India

Sanskriti Pratishthan: *Indian Textiles: An Introduction To The Collection Of Sanskriti Museum Of Indian Textile,* 2011

Singh, Martand; Rta Kapur Chishti and Rahul Jain: *Handcrafted Indian Textiles: Tradition and Beyond,* 2000, Lustre

Tyabji, Laila: *Threads and Voices: Behind the Indian Textile Tradition,* 2007, Marg Publications

Varadarajan, Lotika: *Of Fibre and Loom: The Indian Tradition*, 2008, Manohar Publishers and Distributors

Heritage Education and Communication Service (HECS): Hands on Heritage, 2003, INTACH

HECS: *Adopt A Craft*, 2014, INTACH

HECS: *Care For Heritage*, 2015, INTACH

HECS: *India Unlimited... My Travel Diary, Volume I*, 2019, INTACH

HECS: *India Unlimited... My Travel Diary, Volume II*, 2019, INTACH

HECS: 'Story of Silk' (July-September 2012), *Young INTACH Newsletter*

HECS: 'Cotton the Fabric of India' (July-September 2015), *Young INTACH Newsletter*

HECS: 'India's Weaving Wisdom' (July-September 2019), *Young INTACH Newsletter*

HECS: 'Fibre Fusion' (July-September 2022), *Young INTACH Newsletter*

ONLINE RESOURCES:

https://artsandculture.google.com/story/
https://www.metmuseum.org/toah/hd/intx/hd_intx.htm
https://en.unesco.org/silkroad/countries-alongside-silk-road-routes/india
http://www.vam.ac.uk/content/exhibitions/the-fabric-of-india/textiles-in-a-changing-world/
https://timesofindia.indiatimes.com/
https://www.academia.edu/
https://asiainch.org/
https://indiainch.org/
https://lifestyle.livemint.com/
https://www.britannica.com/topic/
https://en.wikipedia.org
https://www.hindustantimes.com/india/
https://www.bbc.com/news/world-asia-india-37194282
https://www.craftsvilla.com/blog/kanchipuram-silk-sarees-history-weaving-facts/
https://www.textilesphere.com/history-of-indian-textile-industry/
https://museum.gwu.edu/indian-textiles-1000-years-art-and-design
https://www.texmin.nic.in/organisations
https://indiantextilejournal.com/modernisation-indispensable-for-development-of-textile/
https://scroll.in/roving/india
https://fabriclore.com/blogs/journal/history-of-indian-textile
https://www.fibre2fashion.com/industry-article/innovations-to-look-out-for-in-indian-textile-industry
https://journals.sagepub.com/
https://istampgallery.com/headgears-of-india/
https://www.vervemagazine.in/fashion-and-beauty/
https://www.jstor.org/stable/4394405
https://www.thehindu.com/society/
https://www.hindustantimes.com/india/
https://www.thehindu.com/society/
https://outputs.kalgudi.com/p/c/srikalahasti-kalamkari-fabric-painting-of-geethopadesham/4qtc_00zn
https://www.dailypioneer.com/2021/state-editions/
https://www.sarisafari.com/
https://www.indianmirror.com/indian-industries/weaving.html
https://www.sahapedia.org/india

Heritage Education and Communication Service (HECS)

The Indian National Trust for Art and Cultural Heritage (INTACH) is India's largest non-profit membership organisation dedicated to conservation and preservation of India's natural, cultural, living, tangible and intangible heritage.

Recognising the importance of heritage education in spreading awareness among the people, INTACH set up the Heritage Education and Communication Service (HECS) in 1998. Since its inception, HECS is working to create awareness among different target groups such as, the public, professionals, city and local authorities, INTACH chapters, school and college teachers, and students. It designs different types of training programmes to make citizens aware of their role in the conservation and preservation of their natural, cultural and living heritage.

HECS Educational Projects

HECS has developed several innovative projects and programmes in heritage education for school children.

National Teacher Training Workshops

The HECS team in collaboration with INTACH Chapter Convenors conducts workshops on heritage awareness for teachers in different parts of the country. Till date, over 200 workshops have been conducted successfully.

Heritage Clubs

The Heritage Clubs in schools are designed to create awareness and inspire students to participate in heritage-related activities. HECS has a nation-wide network of heritage clubs in around 4000 schools.

Endangered Crafts Workshops

These workshops help spread awareness of an endangered art, craft, and tradition/ practice of a particular region/city by conducting workshops with middle school children.

College Heritage Volunteer Training Programme

A pioneering initiative that aims at sensitising undergraduate college students to protect their heritage and train them to lead a nation-wide movement for heritage conservation and preservation. Since its launch in 2012, over 30 workshops and forums have been organised.

JAGO – Heritage and Citizenship

This workshop presents ways of becoming more informed and active citizens through engagement with heritage by exploring inter-linkages between heritage and citizenship for enthusiastic citizens.

National Outreach Programmes

Our national programmes, like India Heritage Quiz, National Competition, and FilmIt India help nurture cultural understanding, care and concern amongst school children about India's unique and diverse heritage.

Some HECS Publications

Hands on Heritage: A handbook with over 100 activities, worksheets and innovative ideas on learning about India's rich cultural and natural heritage.

A Capital Story: A small booklet on the making of the New Delhi, its architects, how the site was chosen, the design and architectural features of its buildings.

Adopt A Monument: A handbook for teachers, students and enthusiasts who want to learn how to conserve India's magnificent built heritage.

Adopt A Tree: A handbook for teachers, students, and enthusiasts committed to conserve our natural heritage.

Adopt A Craft: A handbook for teachers, students and enthusiasts who want to explore the different crafts practiced in India.

Care For Heritage: This handbook for teachers, students and enthusiasts explains steps for restoration and conservation of art objects or artefacts.

JAGO: Heritage and Citizenship: Presents ways of becoming more active and informed citizens through constructive civic engagement with heritage and support good citizenship initiatives.

Dilli Ki Shaan – Discover Delhi: The book explores Delhi's rich natural, built, and living heritage. These different aspects have been shared in the book along with interesting activities.

The Hornbill Warrior – Know Nagaland (A Colouring Book) (English, Lotha and Ao): This story-cum-colouring book brings out the heritage of Nagaland as discovered through the eyes of a Naga girl.

India Unlimited... My Travel Diary (Vol. 1 & 2): The publication explores India's diverse heritage, covering all of its states and union territories. In this journal, one can record one's travel and cultural and heritage experiences.

Off We Go! Series: These storybooks follow children visiting the cities of Delhi, Kolkata, Mumbai, Jaipur and Chennai during their holidays. While they travel around the cities, they explore the various facets of their heritage.

Teseng Builds a Root Bridge – Know Meghalaya (A Colouring Book) (English and Khasi): This story-cum-colouring book follows the tale of a boy who visits his mother's home state – Meghalaya.

My Little Book on Andaman and Nicobar Islands: The colouring book for primary school children discovers the various forms of heritage of the Andaman and Nicobar Islands – natural, built, living, and also traces its history.

Tree of Life – An Activity Book on Nature Education: It is a comprehensive, informative and colourful handbook for teacher educators, middle school students and natural heritage enthusiasts.

Indian Culture for Everyone (English and Hindi): Indian Culture for Everyone encompasses a wide range of Indian history, presenting the expanse of Indian culture while capturing the essence of the country.

Talking Kitchen: The Talking Kitchen comprises short stories set against the backdrop of the COVID-19 lockdown in March 2020 in India. The write up follows children living in an urban housing society complex and learning about traditional utensils and dishes from their State.

Heritage at Risk: An informative booklet designed to make children aware of India's threatened heritage. The listing of endangered heritage includes natural, built, material, and living heritage.

Chimi in the Magical Land of Kanchendzonga – Know Sikkim (A Colouring Book): This story-cum-colouring book follows the travels of a young girl, Chimi, in her ancestral State of Sikkim. Through the story, she slowly discovers the heritage of Sikkim and realises the need to preserve it.